ON THE

SOUTH AUSTRALIAN

COAST

(INCLUDING KANGAROO ISLAND)

Front Cover: Only the rusted stern of the 711 ton barque *Ethel* remains on the beach bnear Cape Spencer. The dismasted *Hougomont* limps into Port Adelaide, May 1932. (Both Author's Collection).

A PROUDLY AUSTRALIAN BOOK

WRECKS ON THE SOUTH AUSTRALIAN COAST
First Edition 1993

Published by:

An imprint of
OCEANS ENTERPRISES
303 Commercial Road, Yarram, Vic 3971.

National Library of Australia Cataloguing-in-Publication entry:

Loney, J.K. (Jack Kenneth), 1925 -
    Wrecks on the South Australian Coast

    Includes index.
    ISBN 0 646 14744 7
    1. Shipwrecks - South Australia.
    2. Maritime accidents - South Australia.
    I. Title.

919.423

Printed in Australia by Australian Print Group, Maryborough, Victoria.

WRECKS

ON THE

SOUTH

AUSTRALIAN

COAST

INCLUDING KANGAROO ISLAND

Jack Loney

PREFACE

During the two decades of investigation into thousands of shipwrecks around the Australian coast, my research has been at its most invigorating, when after walking hundreds of kilometres of remote beaches and cliffs in search of a greater understanding of the dangers faced by ships' crews and passengers, I have been able to present my findings to interested readers.

In similar vein, venturing to sea with yachtsmen and commercial fishermen, talking with divers and underwater explorers, and visiting the keepers of the few surviving manned lighthouses, also provide a greater appreciation of maritime hazards and a repertoire of fascinating stories, many of which I suspect are probably better told than written.

Early in 1970, while travelling from Apollo Bay in Victoria to Adelaide via the coast road with my young family, we stayed overnight at the Kingston Hotel in the South-east of South Australia to give my children the experience of the night in a typical country hotel.

In the hotel bar I met two lightkeepers from the unique and fascinating Cape Jaffa Lighthouse, at that time already marked for partial dismantling, and I have little doubt that their invitation to visit the lighthouse stimulated my interest in maritime history along the south eastern coastline of South Australia, spawning my first booklet on wrecks in this region the following year.

Over the next few years it was revised and enlarged through four editions to eventually include all major disasters south of Adelaide to the Victorian border, including Kangaroo Island.

I continued my research, intending to cover the entire South Australian coastline, but most of my time was spent locating information for the several volumes of *Australian Shipwrecks*.

Wrecks on the South Coast of South Australia has been out of print for more than a decade, and now *Australian Shipwrecks* has been completed I am able to update details of wrecks in South Australian waters, particularly for the tourist and general interest reader, although divers and maritime historians may find the summary of value.

It is presented briefly without deviation from fact to provide a short account of the disaster, mystery, treachery, endurance, heroism and cowardice contained in the maritime history of the state, and will provide starting points for more comprehensive investigations of particular wrecks.

Jack Loney
Portarlington, 1993.

BIBLIOGRAPHY

References and further reading.

BOOKS

Shipwrecks in South Australia.
Books 1 and 2. (1836-1899); Ronald Parsons.

Shores of Tragedy; Peter Christopher .

South Australian Shipwrecks.
(A Data Base, 1802-1989); Peter Christopher.

Australian Shipwrecks, Volumes 1-5;
Charles Bateson and Jack Loney.

Wrecks on the South Coast Of South Australia,(4 Editions); Jack
Loney.

Australia's Island Shipwrecks; Peter Stone & Jack Loney.

Wrecks at Robe; Jack Loney.

Wrecks in Australian Waters; Jack Loney.

OTHER REFERENCES

South Australian Register.
Adelaide Advertiser.
Sydney Morning Herald.
Australasian Shipping Record.

ACKNOWLEDGEMENTS

Appreciation is expressed to the following who have contributed
photographs and/or written material.
State Library of South Australia, Adelaide.
La Trobe Library, Melbourne.
R.Temme. Adelaide.
R.Parsons. Adelaide.
P. Christopher. Adelaide.
Neil Cormack. Adelaide.
C.E. Perryman. Port MacDonnell.
P.Stone, Yarram,Victoria.
Jill and Igo Oak, Adelaide.
Chris and Cathy Deane, Adelaide.
Stuart Moody, Port Victoria.
Society for Underwater Historic Research.

Authorities were not too concerned when the *Portland Maru* arrived at Port Lincoln in 1935 with a heavy list to starboard but they were soon to rue their complacency as she went down off Cape Torrens, Kangaroo Island. See page 135.
(Photo credits:Top- Author's Collection. Bottom - Adelaide Advertiser).

NOTE ON PHOTOGRAPHS AND ILLUSTRATIONS.

Many of the photographs and illustrations used in this book, obtained from a wide variety of sources since 1956, have been used in some of my previously publications, namely: Australian Shipwrecks, Volumes 2-5; Wrecks in Australian Waters; and Wrecks on South Australia's South East Coast,(four editions.)

All have been acknowledged in good faith, and while many previously believed to exist in only one collection are often discovered elsewhere, making it impossible to trace the source of the originals, I would still be grateful to learn of any errors.

CONTENTS

OTHER TITLES IN THE SERIES:
Wrecks on the New South Wales Coast
Wrecks on the Queensland Coast
IN PREPARATION:
Australia's Island Shipwrecks
ALSO BY JACK LONEY:
Victorian Shipwrecks
The *Loch Ard*

The light on Middle Bank in Spencer Gulf played a major role in the safe movement of shipping to the northern ports. (Department of Transport).

The original lighthouse station at Cape Northumberland, pictured here last century, was eventually demolished and a new light tower erected a short distance away when the eroded cliffs became dangerous and threatened to collapse. (Les Hill).

INTRODUCTION

Over the past century and a half hundreds of fine ships have found their last resting places along the shores of South Australia, and the stories of their loss are closely linked with the settlement and development of the land from Portland in the east to the remote regions of Streaky Bay.

The inlet and river discovered on the eastern side of St. Vincents Gulf in 1831 was the site chosen for the future city of Adelaide in 1836, and within a few years the Port River had been deepened sufficiently to allow vessels up to 500 tons to enter and leave safely.

With the development of the immigrant trade, ships approaching from the west kept a close watch on the notorious Troubridge Shoals which continued to claim many victims after the construction of a lighthouse; particularly among the small craft used to carry produce to market from the ports scattered around Spencer Gulf and further west.

In later years, other lights at Althorpe Island (1879), and South Neptune (1901), lessened the risks to those approaching Adelaide from this direction. On the eastern side, lighthouses on Cape Jervis and Cape Willoughby, supplemented by numerous lesser lights guarded the Backstairs Passage between Kangaroo Island and the mainland for vessels large and small.

The ports of Port Victoria and Wallaroo existed precariously in the early years with supplies arriving by sea from Adelaide at irregular intervals. At Port Victoria, the completion of a long jetty and goods sheds in 1878 opened the way for the arrival of large overseas sailing ships, and grain from surrounding districts was shipped by small steamers and sailing craft to the port where it was loaded into the great windjammers. Wardang Island a short distance off shore provided some shelter for ships waiting to load, but it also became a graveyard for more than twenty vessels, ranging from coastal sail traders and steamers to deep water square riggers.

Following World War 1, sailing ships slipped into relative obscurity but the revival of the annual grain race to Europe in the 1930's gave them a new lease of life and brought renewed prosperity to Port Victoria. The opening of the Wallaroo-Moonta copper fields in 1850 spawned the development of a port at Wallaroo which expanded rapidly, exporting ore and importing all the needs of the mining community. In later years its grain loading facilities expanded and today it is one of the state's major wool and bulk loading ports.

Port Pirie was gradually developed out of a shallow, swampy estuary and soon became a major outlet for nearby wheat growing districts. From 1884 the silver lead mines at nearby Barrier gave great impetus to the expansion of the port and the opening of the rail link with Broken Hill hastened the town's industrial development, with Port Pirie, and nearby Port Germein barely able to keep pace.

Matthew Flinders named Port Lincoln in 1802, then settlers

eventually moved in during 1839. Despite numerous setbacks and relative isolation it has developed into the principal port on the Eyre Peninsula, prominent in grain exports and fishing.

Further west to Streaky Bay, then on to Fowlers Bay, the tiny settlements struggled to maintain regular service from the sea, and most did not show significant development until the early 1900's. After relying heavily on shipping, these days they are serviced overland.

Port Augusta, at the head of the gulf, was used first as a major wool port; then in 1870 became the landing point for the overland telegraph, and was also used to ship minerals.

In December 1800, Grant on board the 50 ton brig *Lady Nelson*, named Capes Banks and Northumberland, Mount Gambier and Mount Schanck, during a voyage out from England, the first land in this area to be seen by an Englishman; then Flinders and Baudin passed by in 1802. However, the close proximity of Kangaroo Island, home of sealers, whalers and scum of the colony, living outside the law would suggest that white men landed on mainland shores many years earlier.

Squatters moved into the district in the 1830's and were soon looking for a suitable port. They favoured Rivoli Bay, but in 1846, a small settlement on the bay named by Baudin in honour of Admiral de Guichen was chosen as the port for immigration and overseas trade. Robe's prosperity increased rapidly in the 1850's when thousands of immigrant Chinese landed there on their way to the Victorian goldfields thus avoiding the ten pounds poll tax imposed by the Victorian Government. In 1857 more than 20,000 landed at Robe, and when this declined wool took over, 8,100 bales being loaded in 1866 alone.

However, immigrant and wool ships were lost in the bay forcing ships' masters to favour Port MacDonnell, Beachport and Kingston, while in later years the larger ships avoided the shallows of Robe's harbour.

Port MacDonnell was officially proclaimed a port in 1860 although the harbour was little more than an open roadstead and vulnerable to gales from the south east, south and south west, reflected in the high toll of ships. Most of the south eastern district shipped wool from here after moorings were laid for large vessels and a jetty constructed. Railways and improvement in roads reduced the commercial value of Port MacDonnell but it is still an important fishing port, and it retains its popularity as a holiday resort.

Along this hostile coast authorities were soon considering likely sites for lighthouses and the establishment of lifeboat and rocket crews. Cape Northumberland lighthouse, built a short distance west of Port MacDonnell in 1859 guarded more than 150 kilometres of coastline before the light at Cape Jaffa was completed in 1872. The Jaffa lighthouse, standing on a platform supported by thirteen screw piles has now been downgraded and replaced by a major light at Robe.

Another important lighthouse stands on Cape Banks. It was built in 1882. some years after the *Admella* was lost on nearby Carpenter Rocks.

To the north west, close by the unique sandhills and back waters of the Coorong, the town of Kingston was founded. Shipping did not call here regularly until the 1860's, but despite the efforts of local businessmen and the construction of a railway to Naracoorte, authorities decided the bay was too shallow and exposed to allow the port to develop for overseas shipping.

Whalers and sealers probably landed on the south coast many years before Flinders and Baudin met in what is now known as Encounter Bay although the first real exploration did not commence until the 1830's when the country back from the coast was examined by land parties.

In 1837 Captain Crozier named Victor Harbour after his vessel *Victor* and about a year later it was proclaimed a port, coming into prominence as a whaling station. However, Port Elliot was favoured more as the main port despite several obvious disadvantages, so moorings were laid out along with a jetty and a small breakwater. Ships bringing passengers and cargo linked with the Murray River paddle steamers which called at Goolwa, but the loss of several vessels brought a decline in trade, and eventually, in 1864 it was replaced by Victor Harbour.

A jetty and moorings were not commenced there until the seventies and then the construction of the railway to Morgan removed its importance as a port for the Murray, although ships continued to call regularly up until World War 1.

Rugged Kangaroo Island, almost astride the main Adelaide to Melbourne shipping lane has been the scene of several of the state's most calamitous shipwrecks. Separated from the mainland by the thirteen kilometre wide Backstairs Passage, the island was first visited by sealers, whalers and outcasts from New South Wales and Van Diemen's Land.

Flinders set foot on the island in 1802 and saw signs which indicated earlier visitors but with much early history clouded in mystery, a legend of stories have grown up around the activities of the first settlers.

Although there have been many wrecks right around the island, a large number of them have been fishing craft and other small vessels. Here again, the foam-edged rollers sweeping on to a barren, rocky coast, alerted the Government of the young colony to many hidden dangers around the island. Cape Willoughby light, overlooking Backstairs Passage was the first built in South Australia. Lit in January, 1852, it was later joined by lights on Capes St.Alban, Borda, and du Couedic, guarding the hidden reefs and shoals.

Loss of the *S.S.Admella* on Carpenter Rocks.
(From the painting by C.Dickson Gregory).

"Turn out, boys"
"What's up with our supper tonight?
The man's mad - Two hours to daylight I'd swear -
Stark mad - why, there isn't a glimmer of light."
"Take Bolingbroke, Alec, give Jack the young mare;
Look sharp. A large vessel lies jammed on the reef,
And many more on board still, and some washed on shore
Ride straight with the news - they may send some relief
From the township; and we - we can do little more."

So runs the first stanza of Adam Lindsay Gordon's famous poem
"From the Wreck", believed to be inspired by the tragic wreck of
S.S.Admella on Carpenter Reef, north west of Cape Northumberland on
6 August, 1859.

CHAPTER ONE

ADMELLA

S.S.Admella (Captain Hugh McEwan) left Port Adelaide early on Friday, 5 August,1859, on her usual run to Melbourne with eighty-one passengers and a crew of twenty-eight. Her cargo consisted of ninety-three tons of copper, flour for the Victorian goldfields, general merchandise and seven horses, four of them racehorses.

Of the passengers, nineteen were women and fifteen children. Three more passengers and one fireman were taken on at Semaphore, making the total complement one hundred and thirteen. The owners of three of the racehorses, Messrs. George and Hurtle Fisher, sons of the President of the South Australian Legislative Council, were among the passengers.

At about 1 p.m., when abreast of Cape Willoughby light on Kangaroo Island, the heavy ocean swell threw the racehorse Jupiter on to his back in his box. While he was being put back on his feet Captain McEwan ordered the ship's bows turned out to sea into the swell and her speed reduced for about an hour. Then she returned to her normal course, steaming parallel to the shore, but further out to sea. By midnight she had covered a further seventy-five miles and although the weather was foggy, her master expected she would make Cape Northumberland before daylight.

All believed the *Admella* to be many miles off-shore, but a few minutes before 5 am she struck a sunken reef with an almost imperceptible bump and the following swell lifted her a further twenty or thirty feet on to the rocks, impelling her with such force that she lay on the summit of the ridge, keeling over with her starboard side high out of the water.

Engines were immediately stopped and for a few seconds the only sound was the crashing of breakers on the rocks. Orders were given to clear the boats, but within fifteen minutes the *Admella* had broken into three sections. First, the funnel crashed down on to one of the lifeboats as the steamer heeled further over, until her beams gave way under the strain. Over the portion of the reef where the midship and fore section lay there was a greater depth of water than where the aft section rested on the reef. Finally, the ship snapped apart at the bulk-heads, bringing down the rigging, chains and blocks and sweeping several passengers and crew into the sea.

The first victims were George Fisher and Dr. Vaux, of Adelaide, also G. Holbrook, who was on his way to England. Perhaps they were the lucky ones. At the same time all the horses were pitched overboard.

Almost all the women and children were on the bow section while more than forty clung to the poop, held reasonably steady by the cargo of copper in the hold. A few rockets were discovered and fired in the hope of attracting the attention of light-keepers at Cape Northumberland, fifteen miles away, but they were damp and failed to ignite correctly. Also discovered were some matches, but these were also practically useless.

Daylight revealed a deserted coastline about a mile away, and plans were being formulated for an attempt to reach shore when a steamer was seen in the distance. Signals were hurriedly erected on the remaining mast and rigging, the ship's bell rung, but the vessel, *Admella's* sister ship *Havilah*, passed without seeing them.

Memorial to the *Admella* on Cape Banks.
(Author's Collection).

Webb, the man in charge of some of the horses, was seen soon after floating on part of a horse box and trying to paddle with his hands, and then another man named Purdon swam off to a piece of timber hoping to get ashore from it. After floating about half a mile away from the wreck the current took them both out to sea.

Next, one of the ship's boats was seen floating keel up close to the wreck and a young Danish seaman named Holm volunteered to swim to it with a line attached to his waist. He reached the boat but the line parted and he spent almost the whole day attempting to avoid being swept out to sea, only to be finally washed off and drowned.

All now realised that their only hope lay in someone reaching the shore and bringing help. The second mate volunteered to swim ashore, but he too disappeared in the raging seas around the reef.

No water could be found in either part of the wreck and there was no food on the fore section. In the poop a piece of ham was located, but all were afraid it would further increase their thirst. However, a small bag of almonds was discovered and doled out.

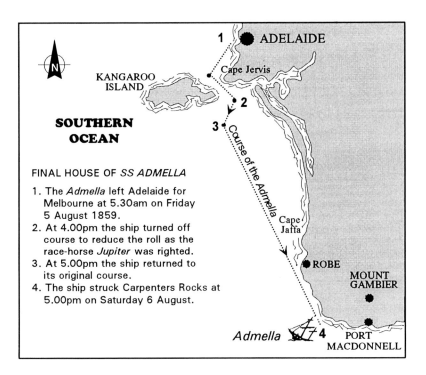

1. ADELAIDE

KANGAROO
ISLAND

Cape Jervis

2

3

SOUTHERN
OCEAN

Course of the Admella

Cape
Jaffa

ROBE

MOUNT
GAMBIER

Admella **4** PORT
MACDONNELL

N

FINAL HOUSE OF SS ADMELLA

1. The Admella left Adelaide for
   Melbourne at 5.30am on Friday
   5 August 1859.
2. At 4.00pm the ship turned off
   course to reduce the roll as the
   race-horse Jupiter was righted.
3. At 5.00pm the ship returned to
   its original course.
4. The ship struck Carpenters Rocks at
   5.00pm on Saturday 6 August.

During the first night on the wreck another ship, *S.S.Bombay*, passed so close that the steady beat of her engines could be heard, but of course there were no rockets, blue lights or lamps to attract attention, and the frantic cries and signals went unnoticed in the dark.

Cold, and drenched with spray, there was further consultation as to who would make the attempt to reach the shore on a raft. Five of the passengers offered £100 each if they were saved, so a decision was made to build a raft next morning.

Survivors on the fore section crossed to the poop during the morning when a rope was finally fastened after many anxious moments. Fifteen men made the crossing, although three men and two children were lost.

No women attempted to cross. They remained with their children and a few of the men also stayed. Their deaths came within a few hours when the forepart broke up.

Sailors set to, making a raft, the only tool available being a meat chopper. The mizzen boom was cut in two and a portion of the main boom was chopped off. These they lashed together and, with a rope fastened to it, they launched the raft overboard with John Leach and Robert Knapman in charge. Captain McEwan told them that if they reached the shore they were to proceed to the Cape Northumberland lighthouse.

The famous Portland lifeboat which played a leading role in the rescue of the few survivors from the *Admella*, at practice in Portland Harbour. After being withdrawn from service it lay neglected in the Portland gardens for many years before being extensively repaired and renovated. It is believed to be the only one of its type remaining. (Author's Collection).

The famous lifeboat used at the wreck of the *Admella* as displayed at Portland for more than sixty years.
(Author's Collection).

For three hours in the afternoon the seamen battled with the breakers as they steered their raft towards the shore. It finally grounded, and in order to save themselves from being carried out again they dived into the sea and dug their hands into the sand, holding on as each succeeding breaker carried them further forward, until they gained the sandy beach. After recovering their strength they signalled to their companions on the wreck, then set out for the lighthouse, struggling all night through swamps and over sandhills. At last they reached the lighthouse and told head keeper B. Germein of the disaster.

Wasting no time, Germein set out for the nearest post office at Mount Gambier on a horse to report the wreck to Adelaide and Melbourne, but he was thrown, and so Peter Black, a local station owner, completed the ride to Mount Gambier.

Within a few hours word of the wreck had spread like wildfire and men and women began converging on the beach opposite the wreck where they found the body of one of the horses and piles of wreckage, including a damaged lifeboat. Three other horses were grazing nearby.

There was no lifeboat closer than Portland, almost two hundred miles away, but Germein arranged for a small boat at the lighthouse to be sent overland by dray. By the time it arrived the damaged ship's lifeboat had been hauled ashore and repaired, although rough seas threatened to delay rescue attempts for at least another day.

By now the sea had gutted all cabins and any places of refuge or shelter, forcing the survivors to climb into the rigging or cling to the side of the hull and steeply angled deck. Meanwhile two fishermen from Robe, and *S.S. Corio* from Adelaide had reached the wreck, but both were powerless in the heavy seas.

Early on Thursday the 11th, Germein attempted to launch his boat, but it too was swamped. Captain Quinn, on the *Corio,* approached close to the wreck and finally decided to launch the pilot boat which she carried. Manned by seven men, it battled the seas for almost an hour before being forced to land on the beach.

The fifty-odd survivors left on the *Admella* set about building yet another raft only to see it also drift away. To add to their miseries those still capable of following the rescue operations saw both boats launched from the beach, then capsized and swamped in the surf.

S.S. Corio, running short of coal, decided to return to Robe but as she left *S.S. Lady Bird* appeared over the horizon from Portland, towing the lifeboat and whaleboat, while *S.S. Ant* also arrived from Robe.

At about 9 a.m. on Friday the lifeboat left the steamer and pulled in to the wreck, approaching from the western or weather side. When only a short distance away two rockets with life lines attached were fired and several attempts to throw a line over the wreck were made, but all failed. Soon after, several huge seas swept over the lifeboat destroying six of the oars and breaking the rudder, but during a lull the exhausted crew succeeded in escaping and returning to the *Lady Bird.*

Captain Fawthrop, captain of the boat, immediately ordered the oars replaced and the boat readied for a second attempt, but found the seas too high and dangerous. Next morning calmer seas enabled Germein in his boat, and the pilot boat, to approach the wreck and fasten a line. One enormous wave took Germein's boat right over the wrecked ship's boiler, but he returned inside it on the crest of the next huge wave. Three of the survivors, Captain McEwan, Thomas Davey and Andrew Fuller managed to haul themselves into Germein's boat and they were then taken aboard the pilot boat and put ashore. In the surf it capsized, but all on board were rescued.

Meanwhile, Germein had rescued another survivor using the *Admella* lifeboat, but this man was drowned when the life boat was also capsized in the surf. The Portland lifeboat and whaleboat, supported by a boat from the *Ant* had now returned and anchored near where they had been the previous day. The bow man in the lifeboat heaved a line over the wreck and after it was fastened eighteen men and one woman were rescued, making the total a mere twenty-four out of the original one hundred and thirteen.

The *Lady Bird* was boarded at about 10 a.m., and after exchanging signals with those on shore she returned to Portland.

At the end of a week's waiting, interest in the wreck had reached fever pitch; and telegraph offices throughout the colonies were crowded, while newspapers printed extra editions only to see them sold out immediately they were released.

A surge of relief swept the country when it was known that the handful of survivors were safe and recovering quickly. For a few weeks crews who had participated in the rescue were treated as heroes, especially Captain Greig and the crew of the *Lady Bird*. When things had quietened down the committees appointed in Melbourne, Adelaide and Portland to handle relief money spent their funds on monetary awards, medals, the publishing of a book dealing with the wreck and a donation to the Sailors' Home.

In Adelaide the committee used its money for monetary awards while those in Portland used the funds to pay accounts for lodging and for clothing the survivors; also doctors' bills and other sundries associated with their care once they were landed at Portland. The medals were eventually presented by the Governor at a function in the Exhibition Building, Melbourne, on 25 June, 1860.

A Commission appointed to inquire into the loss of the *Admella* decided the principal cause was a strong inshore current, adding that the *Bombay* was probably fortunate not to suffer a similar fate. More efficient means of inserting watertight bulkheads were needed as they had contributed to the premature destruction of the vessel and heavy loss of life. Captain McEwan was cleared of any blame but was criticised for not taking regular soundings when uncertain of his position.

And what became of the remains of the *Admella?* Late in August goods salvaged or washed ashore were auctioned on the beach opposite the wreck and a week later her remains and the cargo brought £850. Subsequent salvage attempts were not a total success as the ship, in breaking up, had made recovery of the valuable copper difficult and the ocean was seldom very calm.

In 1860 the remains were sold again to R. Anderson, of Mount

This signal cannon was installed at the Cape Banks when the lighthouse when erected and manned in 1882 to warn of Carpenter Rocks. The light was converted to automatic operation in 1928. The plaque beside the gun reads: "Signal cannon formerly in use at Cape Banks Lighthouse. The "Admella", subject of Adam Lindsay Gordon's peom "The Ride From The Wreck" was wrecked near Cape Banks in 1859".

Gambier, and H. Chant, who then set about recovering more material. Before disposing of the remains Anderson used some materials recovered to build a cottage at Port MacDonnell.

Gradually the wreck almost drifted from memory until 1957 when skindivers recovered copper, and after forming a syndicate, raised more than 250 tons of the metal.

The *Admella* has left us many interesting relics. For years metal plates from the ship were used to reinforce and secure crumbling walls in the Robe gaol. The maritime museum at Port MacDonnell has a restored signal cannon from her, many items from the ship, pieces of cargo, and an excellent display of photographs. Local residents could direct visitors to the cottage built by Anderson using wreckage from the ship. At Cape Banks a cairn commemorates the wreck, and at Cape Northumberland near the site of the early lighthouse is a memorial commemorating the deeds of head light keeper Germein who played a prominent role in the rescue. Of course we must not forget the famous lifeboat used by Fawthrop and his gallant crew, still on display at Portland.

And yet, even today, some questions remain unanswered. What became of the supposed treasure carried by passenger James Wittaker, who lost his life. And Gordon's poem, "From the Wreck" - is it really a description of Black's ride to Mount Gambier with news of the disaster?

Built at Glasgow and brought out under canvas in 131 days, *S.S.Admella* was refitted at Port Adelaide before embarking on her maiden voyage to Melbourne.

Shipping reporters of the day enthusiastically lauded her splendid appearance, construction and fittings, and in the "Adelaide Observer" and "South Australian Register" she was described as a "very beautiful specimen of naval architecture".

Her hull was long and low with a female figurehead crowned with a wreath of wheat, the ears of which formed a tiara to represent the cereal production of the colonies. The stern was elliptical and ornamented with carvings in keeping with ship design of that period. The main saloon, forty feet long, was well decorated, carpeted and furnished, and featured telescopic dining tables extending down the centre. On each side were settees with folding backs.

Well-fitted enclosed cabins extended for part of the way down each side of the vessel and there was also a library containing about 100 volumes. Second class passengers were accommodated near the fore-hold with a separate cabin for women passengers and iron-framed bunks. The lower holds under the fore and aft cabins could hold almost 500 tons of cargo.

Safety equipment included four lifeboats, two pairs of lifebelts and twelve swimming belts. Another special safety feature which was later to bring about the total destruction of the *Admella* and hasten the loss of life was the provision of watertight bulkheads riveted to the hull and dividing the ship into three watertight compartments. The holes for the hundreds of rivets around the hull to hold each bulkhead in place weakened the metal so that it was unable to withstand the enormous stresses placed upon it as the ship was battered by heavy seas.

The engines were placed aft and the boilers forward and the coal bunkers, with a capacity of 100 tons, were between. She was rigged as a three-masted schooner, for all steamers of the period carried sail to supplement their steam power, which was still relatively primitive compared with later steam-driven vessels. However, her top speed, using her engines and sail, was estimated to be almost twenty knots.

Samuel Mossman, in his "Narrative of the Shipwreck of the Admella," printed and published for the Committee of the Admella Fund in 1859, passed these comments on the vessel:

"Of the class of vessels to which the *Admella* belonged, it may be said that although not the largest in number and tonnage employed in the inter-colonial trade, still it is the most important in passenger traffic. Not only do they equal the most improved boats of the British in build and speed, but they excel them in their internal arrangements for comfort and luxury. To those in the mother country who have seen the screw steamers that ply between England and the Continent, or up the Mediterranean, with their luxurious accommodation, they will realise some idea of their appearance and the class of passenger traffic. As the wreck of a British passenger steam vessel is almost certain to involve the loss of influential individuals well known in the circles of the trading ports, thereby augmenting the melancholy interest of such a catastrophe, so the wreck of an inter-colonial steamer with loss of passengers and crew, creates more sensation among the several communities of the Australian colonies, than that of the largest foreigner. "

The *Admella* was an iron, single screw steamer of 392 tons, built at Glasgow in 1857 on dimensions of 193 x 24 x 14 feet.

Awards granted to rescuers at the wreck of the *Admella*.

Life Boat Crew and their Awards:
    Captain: J. Fawthrop (Gold medal and £100)
    Coxswain: W. Rosevear (Silver medal and £50)
    Crew: W. Booth, A. Carey, J. Dumond, J. Dusting, P. Francis, W. Guy, J. Kean, W. Kirkin, H. McDonald, C. Patterson, T. Tweedale, T. Ward, J. Oustney (all received Silver medals and awards ranging from £25 to £12/10/-.)

Whale Boat Crew and their Awards:
    Headsman: J.Cambray (Silver medal and £25).
    Crew: W.Wright, W.King, J.Morgan, G.Scoffal, J. Spiers (all received Silver medals and £12/10/-.)

Additional Awards:
    The sum of £200 was distributed to the captains and crews of the steamers *Corio* and *Ant* - £100 to each vessel.

Lists of amounts voted for the relief of survivors and their dependents:
    The widow and family of Captain Harris, the passenger who dived for provisions in the submerged cabin of the Admella - £200.
    Mrs. Jackson, the widow of a passenger who was lost with a large sum of money on his person - £100.
    Mrs.Hermann, whose husband was lost, and who was left in destitute circumstances - £100
    Miss Ledwith, the only female survivor - £50.
    Hugh McInnes,a ship's carpenter, and passenger on the ill-fated vessel, who lost a sum of money and his tools - £50.
    Henry Short, who lost his wife and four children, besides a quantity of furniture - £50.
    E. Underwood, a master mariner, and father of a lad among the lost passengers who was entrusted with his nautical instruments - £25.
    Charles Lock, a survivor - £20.
    John McDermott, second cook on board the *Admella* - £20.

Also, £50 was awarded to the parent, or any relative of the brave Soren Holm, who lost his life in endeavouring to secure the ship's lifeboat.

Many of the men who assisted at the rescue also received from London, the Board of Trade bronze medal for "Gallantry in Saving Life at Sea" and also the Shipwrecked Fishermen's and Mariner's Royal Benevolent Society's Silver medal for "Heroic Exertion in Saving Life from Drowning. "

Many interesting relics have been recovered from the remains of the illfated *Admella.* These include a bell and porthole, and a magnificently restored signal cannon (see *A Cannon Surrenders*). (Port MacDonnell Maritime Museum).

FAWTHROP AND GERMEIN

The tragic wreck of the *Admella* brought together briefly two outstanding men who took prominent roles in early maritime developments in south eastern Australia.

The town of Portland is proud to remember its famous Harbour Master, Captain James Fawthrop. For almost two decades Fawthrop took a leading role in the rapid development of the port: landing place for immigrants, base for whalers and haven for seamen from all corners of the globe. Born at Plymouth, England in 1804 he made his first voyage to Australia as chief officer of a ship bringing convicts to Van Diemen's Land in 1829. During this voyage the master died and Fawthrop took command. He returned for the second time in 1834 and then for fifteen months served with the pilots at Tamar Heads.

In 1835 he took command of the brig *Eagle* and two years later carried sheep from Tasmania to Portland Bay for the Hentys. He next

Captain James
Fawthrop, Portland
Harbour Master - he
took a leading role in
the rescue of *Admella*
survivors.
(Portland Harbour
Trust and Port
Adelaide Maritime
Museum, 1974).

commanded their schooner *Minerva*, then the brig *Julia Percy*, before transferring to the brig *City of Sydney* in 1849.

In 1853 Fawthrop was appointed Harbour Master at Portland and for fifteen years gave excellent service. His carefully compiled records have left historians a well documented description of an important period in the port's history.

In addition to the routine running of the port, Fawthrop organised rescue crews which attended wrecks close to Portland, but he achieved most fame in 1859, following the rescue of survivors from the *Admella*.

Fawthrop and his lifeboat crew were to be involved in two more local wrecks before he retired. In 1863, when the barque *Jane* ran ashore at Cape Bridgewater, Fawthrop despatched the boat to the scene under the command of the coxswain then proceeded overland. Two months later the full crew attended the wreck of the brig *Julia* near the Fitzroy River. They rescued the passengers and crew but unfortunately a whale boat supporting them was capsized and five of her crew drowned.

Fawthrop retired on half pay in 1868 and died ten years later.

When recounting the story of the *Admella* disaster, historians often gloss over the part played by Benjamin Germein, at the time of the wreck Head Keeper at the Cape Northumberland lighthouse. Germein, born in 1826, was the youngest of three sons; all seamen, who captained ships in South Australian waters and later became pilots. Among the ships in which he served were the *Meander, Lapwing, Lubra, Corio, Emma Sharrott,* and *South Australian.*

When stationed in the pilot service at Semaphore he followed the custom of the day, when pilots sailed their cutters out as far as the Neptune Islands to meet incoming ships and pilot them to their anchorages or berths. Germein's masterly seamanship often enabled him to sail many of the large ships right into port still under canvas and for years early residents spoke of the time in 1852 when he took the 1,600 ton rigged ship *Cleopatra* right in to her anchorage in the North Arm at Port Adelaide. He was also the first captain to take a large vessel through the treacherous mouth of the Murray and made several trips in to Goolwa and out again in command of the steamer *Corio.* He also spent some time as master of the Government schooner *Yatala,* before taking up the position of light keeper at Cape Northumberland, with the added responsibility of selecting and surveying a port to serve the Mount Gambier district.

On the evening of 21 October 1861, the brig *John Omerod,* on a voyage from Adelaide to Sydney with a cargo of flour was struck by a heavy squall when south of Cape Northumberland. Several of her crew were washed away and drowned, leaving the captain and two seamen lashed to the hulk as she drifted to within sight of the lighthouse.

Germein visited her and recovered the body of the steward who had been trapped in the saloon and drowned when the vessel first heeled over in the squall. Earlier, Germein had set the seal on his reputation as an outstanding and fearless seaman with his organisation of and participation in the attempts from the shore to rescue passengers and crew from the *Admella* as she lay on Carpenter Rocks.

While rescuing survivors from the *John Omerod,* Germein lost several fingers when the pilot boat was thrown against the brig but remained at the lighthouse for several more years until his love of the sea lured him back to the pilot service. As steam replaced sail he lost much sympathy and respect for the service, grumbling that any dredge master or hopper skipper could navigate the river in a steamer, while it took a very smart fellow to work up a big sailing craft.

Sometimes, towards the end of his career he would take a solitary voyage out to sea, but being such a skilled boatman his absence caused little concern. On one occasion he was alone for six weeks cruising among the remote Sir Joseph Banks Group in Spencer Gulf.

Ben Germein,
lighthouse keeper,
also took a leading
role in the rescue
of *Admella*
survivors.
(Portland Harbour
Trust and Port
Adelaide Maritime
Museum, 1974).

Early in 1891 he disappeared after writing letters to his family and
the President of the Marine Board stating that he intended committing
suicide. Search parties eventually found him in Shell Creek, near
St.Kilda, north of Port Adelaide. He left again in May 1893 but
returned after being absent for a fortnight. On 3 July he disappeared
again, and after a lengthy search his body was discovered in the
mangroves on Bog Island on 19 September. Troubled in mind, he had
apparently taken his own life.

On 30 December 1944, a memorial seat was unveiled near the
remains of the first lighthouse erected on Cape Northumberland as a
tribute to the bravery and heroism of a pioneer seaman.

A CANNON SURRENDERS

David Leslie with his magnificently restored *Admella* cannon.
Leslie also made the gun carriage.
(Photo: P.Stone.Seadive).

The inflexibility and bureaucratic attitudes of officials administering both the Commonwealth and State Historic Shipwreck Acts in the immediate years after they were proclaimed was clearly illustrated in author Peter Stone's article in the magazine *Skindiving in Australia*, summarised below.

On 17th January, 1982, Victorians David Leslie and Peter Mead recovered an 80 kilogram brass cannon from the site of the wreck of S.S.Admella. David spent more than 10 hours cleaning off over a century of marine growth, restoring the brass to its original gleaming gold. Meanwhile, a wood and brass carriage modelled on an exact half scale replica of the carriages on *H.M.S. Victory* was constructed, and the cannon was first displayed at the "Oceans 83" Congress in Melbourne. The relic had been declared, as required by the Navigation Act 1912-1929 and the recently introduced Historic Shipwreck Act 1981

(South Australia), but no acknowledgment was received from the Department of Home Affairs and Environment at Canberra.

David Leslie retained custody of the cannon for three years, and then in 1986 he received a request from J.C.Womersley of the South Australian Department of Environment and Planning to obtain it for display during South Australia's Jubilee Year. No mention was made of permanent acquisition but David believed that if this eventuated he would be eligible for a reward. However, in their communications the South Australian State Heritage Branch apparently showed little concern for the cost of transport, insurance, security, and the return of the cannon, and in later communications both they and the Commonwealth indicated that he pay for transport and insurance; and there was no mention of the specially made carriage.

David Leslie did not comply with their demands and continued to negotiate through his solicitor until a notice appeared in the Commonwealth of Australia Gazette dated 15th January, 1988, demanding total possession. There was no mention of a reward as allowed by the Act, or compensation for the estimated $5000 spent on its recovery and restoration.

Despite more negotiations, the final blow came in March 1988 when David Leslie received a Supreme Court Writ demanding that he hand over the cannon. More correspondence followed and finally on 12th October, 1988, David's solicitor received a settlement notice from the Australian Government Solicitor which stated (in summary).
1. Discontinuance of the Supreme Court action.
2. A plaque placed with the cannon on display acknowledging Leslie and Mead.
3. A reward of a "reasonable sum".
4. S.A. Government to pay for transport and storage.
5. Mr Leslie to deliver the cannon to the Commonwealth.
6. Mr Leslie acknowledges that the Commonwealth owns the cannon.
7. Mr Leslie releases the Government for any claims of compensation.
8. That each party bears the costs of the Supreme Court Action.

David Leslie settled for a $3500 reward and the cannon eventually went on show at the Port MacDonnell Maritime Museum.

The *Loch Vennachar,* another Loch Line ship lost on Kangaroo Island. She over ran her distance on the way out to Adelaide from London in 1905.

CHAPER TWO
LOCH VENNACHAR

The disappearance of the full rigged iron clipper *Loch Vennachar* with her crew of 26 during a voyage from London to Adelaide, then Melbourne, is one of Australia's most intriguing marine mysteries.

Built in 1875, the *Loch Vennachar* averaged 85 days for twelve passages between London and Melbourne and always made good time on the run home with wool. She also had her share of misfortune.

In June 1872, she was dismasted during a cyclone in the southern Indian Ocean and after reaching Mauritius under jury rig, finally arrived in Melbourne after a voyage of 250 days.

The Melbourne Argus dramatically reported:

"Two enormous waves bore down upon the ship, which rode slowly over the first, and sank to an interminable depth in the trough at the other side. Whilst in this position the second wave came on, towering half-way up the foremast, and broke on board, filling the lower topsail 60 feet above the deck, as it came.

Hundreds of tons of water swept over the ship in a solid mass from stem to stern, thundering inboard on the port side of the foc's'le and racing away over the main deck and over the poop, where most of the crew were standing. Every man on the poop was thrown down, and when they regained their feet they perceived that the formast and mainmast were over the side, and the mizzen topmast above their heads had disappeared. Not a man on board actually saw the spars go or even heard the crash of the breaking rigging, so violent was the shock and so fierce the howling of the hurricane. The cook was washed out of his galley and swept overboard, the galley being completely gutted of everything it contained."

Bound for South Australia on what turned out to be her last voyage out to Australia, she was sighted by *S.S. Yongala* on 6 September 1905, 160 miles west of the Neptune Islands, about four days out of Port Adelaide.

Captain Rees, of the *Yongala,* later reported:

"We saw a ship under full sail at 10 o'clock in the forenoon of September 6th, about 160 miles west of the Neptune Islands, as we were making for Port Adelaide from Fremantle. The weather was fine and clear, the wind gentle from the south-east. As we approached the ship they hoisted signals asking what was the longitude, to which we responded giving the desired information. Subsequently the ship again made signals which we could not distinguish. The course of the Yongala was accordingly altered to bring her close to the ship, when the signals were made out to be "Loch Vennachar, please report me all well".

A composite photograph, prepared after the *Loch Vennachar* was lost with her crew in 1905. One item of interest is the photograph of Tom Pearce Junior, Apprentice Seaman, in the bottom left. He was one of the sons of Tom Pearce, famous as the hero of the *Loch Ard* wreck near Port campbell (Victoria) in 1878. (Author's Collection).

We afterwards went so near to the Loch Vennachar that we could make out her name quite easily on the stern, and a number of persons were also plainly to be seen on the decks of the ship. Three or four men, one of whom I took to be Captain Hawkins, were standing on the poop, near the man at the wheel, but whether there were passengers aboard we could not tell. It is not improbable that the mate and second mate were on the poop with the captain. The *Loch Vennachar* was then heading about E.N.E., the course of her destination.

As we again proceeded on our way the man whom we took to be Captain Hawkins waved an adieu as he still stood on the vessel's poop. The *Loch Vennachar*, judging by her appearance, seemed to have had generally a fine voyage, and presented a pretty sight, as with her sails in full standing she sped along with every apparent prospect of shortly reaching port safely."

When the **Loch Vennachar** was reported overdue the Government steamer *Governor Musgrave* left to search for her on 18 September, but was unsuccessful.

Anxiety for the **Loch Vennachar** first surfaced when the press reported in Adelaide on Friday 22nd:
*"The steamer Governor Musgrave returned today from her search for signs of the overdue ship **Loch Vennachar**. The coast of Kangaroo Island was examined, and also that of smaller islands on the south coast. No signs of recent wreckage were discovered. In shipping circles the gravest fears are now entertained regarding the safety of the vessel."*

More than two months later, on 2 December the Adelaide Observer said:
"The finding of a body and piles of wreckage in the vicinity of West Bay seems now to indicate that the ship struck on the western side of the island. It is evident that the hull is now breaking up and releasing cargo which was before held in the wreck. The further result of Mounted Constable Thorpe's search will be awaited with interest, and should he succeed in definitely locating the wreck he will perform an important service."

Although wreckage continued to come ashore for several months, the wreck was never located. The whisky casks were eventually shipped back to Adelaide, and the **Loch Vennachar** lay almost forgotten for more than half a century - another mystery of the sea.

In 1976, three divers, Brian Marfleet, Doug Seton and Terry Smith, all members of the South Australian Society for Underwater Historical Research, discovered the remains of the **Loch Vennachar** just north from the entrance into West Bay, lying in about eight fathoms, below 100-foot cliffs. Their find paved the way for a major expedition of thirty-four persons - divers, surveyors, museum staff, draughtsmen,

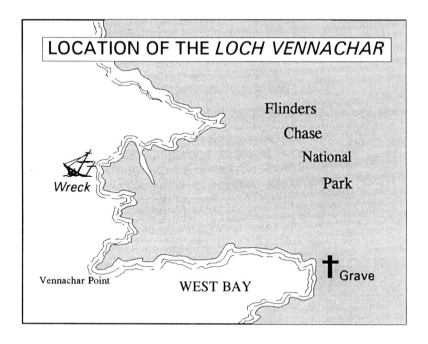

LOCATION OF THE *LOCH VENNACHAR*

Flinders

Chase

National

Park

Wreck

Vennachar Point

WEST BAY

✝ Grave

climbers and cooks.

After rough seas had restricted operations for more than a week divers located a bow section rammed into an underwater crevice, surrounded by twisted and broken ship's plates. Pig iron lay widely scattered; there were portholes and the base of a mast. In the remains of the chain lockers divers found some chain, still coiled, and seven anchors. One, about twelve feet long, was estimated to weigh about five tons. Other relics recovered included bricks, a fairlead and remains of a winch.

The mystery surrounding the disappearance of the **Loch Vennachar** had been solved. Before returning to Adelaide the expedition placed a tablet commemorating the ship and her crew in the cliffs overlooking the wreck site. Its extreme remoteness, and the heavy seas which roll in almost continuously, will ensure that the remains of this once splendid vessel will lie relatively undisturbed forever.

The following letter, written at "Torture Camp", West Bay, Kangaroo Island, on Saturday, 9-12-05, by Trooper Thorpe, dramatically illustrates the difficulties in locating shipwrecks off remote regions.

Doubtless you have seen in the papers the result of my visit of inspection to the Shipwreck Shelter Hut at this bay, and the sad

Hull ribs and beams lie in a junk-yard pile on the site of the *Loch Vennachar.* (Photo courtesy Society for Underwater Historical Research).

discovery we made - I had a man named May with me for company, as it is both a rough, scrubby and dangerous place to come to alone. He is a farmer living 15 miles from here. We first visited the Cape De Condie (Du Couedic) shelter shed two days previous to coming to this one and found all the stores, etc., intact.

On Sunday, the 26th November, we rode to this bay and tied our horses up at this creek where I have pitched my camp. We walked to the beach through dense scrub for a mile. My mate was walking some distance from the creek whereas I was keeping close to the bank, and after going nearly half a mile I called out, "Hullo, there's some casks from the Loch Vennachar."

He came to me, and as we walked towards the mouth of the creek where it empties into the sea, we saw casks all over the beach, some full, some three-quarters full, some half and quarter full of whisky. A lot of it was "Vanguard" whisky in 18 gallon casks; also a hogshead full of English draught ale, also some casks of "Taymouth" whisky, also some casks of "McPhersons" whisky (36 gallon), also some casks of "Bon Accord" whisky, also some "Dewars" whisky, also one cask of oil. All were consigned to Melbourne.

There were also a number of casks of whisky consigned to Adelaide firms. Also a host of bales of paper, same as this piece I have written this letter on. There are a lot of reels of greenish blue paper consigned to the "Observer" Office, Adelaide; it is the coloured paper they generally use for the cover of their weekly paper "The Observer". Loose tins of "Davidson's" tinned fish is also strewn all over the place. We found two casks intact; they are consigned to a Melbourne firm. Such articles as hair brushes, clothes brushes, brooms, etc., are also to be found, and pipes that have been smoked out of, pieces of flannel, under shirts, and under pants, white linen shirts, pieces of serge, and tweed trousers with pieces of braces attached, also pieces of ladie's (sic) underclothing marked "B. Patterson" and a man's sock marked "J. H. Patterson". The last named two articles were part of Captain Patterson's (deceased) effects which Captain Hawkins was bringing out for Mrs Patterson. She came to Melbourne in one of the mail liners, her husband had died aboard his sailing ship en route to England - and as Captain Hawkins of the Loch Vennachar was a great personal friend of Captain and Mrs Patterson, he promised to bring the late Captain's effects out and probably she put some of her own underclothing in the same boxes, which accounts for them washing up.)

"There are also two 60-foot spars and a number of smaller ones, all chewed about by the rocks, which are very sharp on either side of the bay. There are piles of wreckage from almost every part of the ship; cabin doors, legs of tables, settees, pillows, mattresses. Some of the wreckage is to be found in crevices and on ledges of rocks over twenty feet from the level of the sea, showing clearly what a dreadful sea there must have been the night or day the poor old gallant "Vennachar" met her fate. I can quite understand why it is none of the poor fellows reached shore alive. The rocks would chop them to pieces, so sharp and hard are they, besides this coast is teeming with sharks, and the sea that must have been running then, why nothing could live in it. We have some dreadful seas off our southern and south-west coast. The island is one continuous formation of high rugged cliffs over 350 feet in many places and a straight drop into the seething waters. There are heavy pieces of the ship's bulwarks over 20 feet long, with the top rail and sides and great heavy iron stays attached. The spars have long pieces of wire rope and heavy iron hooks, etc., attached. I gather from these that the ship must have struck a sunken rock not far out from the mouth of West Bay because such terribly heavy wreckage could not possibly float far. The ship has probably been dismasted during the terrible weather she met and drifted inshore. It is only twelve miles to the south of Cape Borda lightilouse.

We then turned our eyes to the north end of the beach, and seeing something dark lying on the sand just near the shelter hut, I said to my mate, "I believe that's a body." We could not tell for certain owing to the distance. We however drew nearer and there we found the de-composed body of a poor young fellow, probably not more than 17 or 18. It smelled awfully bad. It was lying on its back, the skin was dry, all the features were completely gone and the flesh was leaving the skull; the left leg was thrown clean across the body and was almost detached at the hip joint. The right leg and arms were somewhat naturally shaped, they did not appear to be as shrunken as the left leg. It was a rather prettily shaped body, being slight yet compact, about 5 ft 7 or 8, remarkably tiny hands and feet (more like a female), the teeth were evidently perfect, no hair or clothing. It was too much decomposed to get a good description.

My mate and I carried the body up to a flat and buried it in its lonely grave, without a friendly tear, except our own. It is a dreadfully lonely place, high towering sand hummocks, and cliffs, and dense scrub, which made our sad task ever so much harder. The place, save for the roaring waves, is as still as death. I got a brass tipped capstan bar and nailed a cross piece on to form a cross, and with the aid of a stick and a tin of black paint recovered from the wreck, I marked on the cross, "Body from Loch Vennachar 26-11-05."

Since then the Government has appointed me Receiver of Wrecks for Kangaroo Island, and as I have recovered 44 casks of whisky etc. (majority full), I must remain in this terribly lonely camp for God knows how long; anyway until a vessel can get in the bay to take it away. It will be a risky job whoever takes it on. I shall be glad to get home to my family again - 30 miles away.

We have to live on wallaby and damper and black tea made from brackish water. I left home on Wednesday 22nd November and am here in camp still. I have had a terribly rough job of late riding and walking over the terribly rugged cliffs and through dense scrub; I have at times been fairly dead beat. I have secured you some nice pieces of wood and will forward them to you as soon as I get home.

Yours faithfully,
(Signed) R.C.Thorpe, Mounted Constable.

The Marine Board steamer *Governor Musgrave* which attended many wrecks on the South Australian coast.
(SSL:M:B11013)

Built at the entrance to Port Adelaide in 1867 to replace a lightship, the Port Adelaide lighthouse became a well known landmark until replaced by the Wonga Shoal light in 1901, when it was re-erected on South Neptune Island. It served there until replaced again in 1985 and now stands in the grounds of the South Australian Maritime Museum.
(Department of Transport).

CHAPER THREE
CHRONOLOGICAL LIST OF WRECKS

1837

Severe gales destroyed two vessels in Encounter Bay during December. Both were lost in Rosetta Harbour which was exposed to severe southerly weather for most of the year.

Captain McFarlane in the *South Australian*, 236 tons, anchored off the harbour for almost a fortnight awaiting the arrival of the brig *Solway*, was finally caught in a southerly gale, blown from her moorings, then driven over a reef. The passengers and crew were fortunate to escape with their lives but the vessel soon went to pieces.

A few days later the *Solway* and *John Pirie* arrived and anchored near where the *South Australian* had been lost. Another severe southerly gale sprang up and both were driven ashore. Several attempts to refloat the *Solway* failed and she eventually became a total wreck, but the *John Pirie* was refloated from the same reef that had destroyed the *South Australian*.

One tragedy caused indirectly by the wreck of the *South Australian* was the drowning of Judge Sir John Jeffcott near the mouth of the Murray. He was on his way to Van Diemen's Land aboard the *South Australian* when she was lost. While waiting for the *John Pirie*, he joined a party of men exploring the river mouth. Their whaleboat was swamped by a roller, drowning Jeffcott, Captain Blenkinsop, manager of the whaling station at Victor Harbour, and two other men.

Built in 1819 as the *Marquis of Salisbury*, the *South Australian* served in the Royal Navy between 1824 and 1836 as *H.M.S. Swallow*, until purchased by the South Australian Company and renamed.

The *Solway* was a vessel of 337 tons, built in 1829 and also owned by the South Australian Company.

1838

Troubridge Shoal on the western side of St Vincent's Gulf has always menaced shipping approaching or leaving Port Adelaide, and the wooden brig *Dart* became its first major victim when she went ashore there on the night of 29 March. At low tide she lay in about a metre of water, leaking badly, and by the following day had heeled over and become a total wreck. There was no loss of life and the crew returned to Holdfast Bay a couple of days later. Built at Sunderland in 1818, the *Dart* was a vessel of 108 tons, registered in Sydney.

Rough weather off the South Australian coast during June battered two vessels.

The schooner *Fanny,* bound from Hobart to Swan River with passengers and a general cargo ran ashore near Cape Jaffa on 22 June while the *Elizabeth* which had sailed from Adelaide to Launceston was driven aground in Rivoli Bay.

The crew of the *Fanny* fought desperately to save her but she drove broadside on to the beach where she was swept by giant seas. A line was fastened to the shore and all soon reached safety where friendly aboriginals helped them light fires and showed the location of permanent waterholes. After several attempts to reach the whaling station at Encounter Bay they met up with men from the *Elizabeth* and eventually all reached safety.

The *Elizabeth* was eventually salvaged and returned to Adelaide for refitting. Two men who journeyed overland to the *Fanny* to recover valuables were not seen again and were presumed to have been killed by aborigines.

The cutter *William,* 20 tons, was driven ashore and lost in Aldinga Bay in August.

The barque *Parsee,* bound from Hobart to Adelaide became another victim of the Troubridge Shoal when she went ashore there on 17 November. Within a week she was a total loss and very little of her cargo was recovered undamaged. Her twenty-seven passengers were taken to Port Adelaide on the *Rapid.* Built at Dumbarton in 1831, the *Parsee* was a wooden vessel of 349 tons, registered at London.

1839

The brig *David Whitton* had delivered sheep from Port Phillip and was returning from Adelaide for another consignment when she went ashore south of the entrance to the Onkaparinga River during a gale on 17 March. Although she became a total loss the crew reached safety and some of her cargo was saved. Built in 1833, the *David Whitton* was a wooden vessel of 271 tons registered at London.

Aborigines stalked and massacred survivors from the brig *Maria,* 136 tons, after she was wrecked on the Coorong early in July. She left Adelaide for Hobart with twenty-seven passengers and crew, also a mixed cargo which included a quantity of sovereigns, but shortly after sailing adverse weather forced her ashore on the barren sandy coast. All reached safety with an ample supply of clothing and provisions, and after a hasty conference, decided to follow the beach back to Encounter Bay where they knew help could be obtained.

Friendly natives guided them over the first part of their long walk, but when they split up following a dispute over the best route to follow, hostile natives who had remained hidden swooped down on them, killing every man, woman and child. News of the massacre eventually reached Encounter Bay and an expedition under Captain Pullen left to investigate the report and look for survivors. The wreck was located,

Police Inspector
Alexander Tolmer who
led a well armed force
which captured and
punished the
aborigines responsible
for the murder of
survivors from the
Maria.
(SSL:M:B6851).

and after a short search, bodies of some of the victims were uncovered.

The party returned immediately and troopers were despatched to round up all aborigines in the area. This was accomplished after some trouble and two of the killers were hanged before the assembled tribe. Some of the sovereigns, buried near the wreck were recovered but a few still believe that a hidden fortune lies buried in the drifting sands of the Coorong, awaiting some lucky finder.

The *Maria* was built in 1823. Dim: 70.2ft x 21ft x 10.9ft.

The wreck of a schooner discovered in Aldinga Bay in August was presumed to be that of the *Emma* after casks branded with the name were discovered. However no vessel named *Emma* was ever reported missing around the South Australian coastline, so perhaps she had been lost well out to sea.

The memorial to the *Maria*, lost on a reef assumed to be the Margaret Brock, in 1840, standing near the mouth of Maria Creek at Kingston, was unveiled before a crowd of about 1,500 on 18 February 1966. (Author's Collection).

The cutter *Frances*, 7 tons, left Memory Cove on a sealing voyage in August but was wrecked on an island at the entrance to Spencer Gulf. The survivors existed miserably for several weeks until rescued by a party from Port Lincoln.

References to the loss of the *Rivals* have been difficult to locate. Some old Australian Directories of last century mention her as striking the Margaret Brock Reef, while the Australian Encyclopedia says she was wrecked to the west of Cape Bernouilli (Cape Jaffa) about 1840. This appears to be one of those unsubstantiated wrecks often reported around the Australian coastline early century.

1843

The sloop *Ranger,* 8 tons, may have been lost in Encounter Bay.

The Hobart whaler *Camilla* met bad weather off the South Australian west coast and after taking shelter in Streaky Bay with two anchors down, was eventually driven ashore on 27 April when they parted.

The crew reached safety and landed her stores and whaling gear before carrying out repairs. The mate was sent to Launceston to charter a vessel to help save the *Camilla* while the crew camped on the beach and went bay whaling.

Some maritime history researchers believe the story of the wreck of the *Camilla* provides the basis of the apparently fictitious account of the wreck of the whaler *Carib.* In 1859 a seaman named William Jackman published an autobiography titled "The Australian Captive" and in it described a voyage he made in a whaler *Carib* in 1837. Jackman claimed that the vessel was forced ashore by a gale on the Great Australian Bight with the loss of five lives. Captured soon after by a Nullarbor tribe he was separated from his twenty-six companions and remained a captive for almost two years. No official records exist to confirm his story which concludes with his rescue by crewmen from the whaler *Camilla.*

Built in 1827 the *Camilla* was a brig of 262 tons, registered at Hobart Town.

The cutter *Kate,* 15 tons, broke her moorings in Spencer Gulf one night in June while the crew were ashore and stranded high on the beach. She could not be refloated.

This was how an artist imagined castaway William Jackman must have looked after he escaped from aborigines on the Nullabor Plain. Jackman, then eighteen, had been a captive for almost two years and his story may have been linked with the wreck of the whaler *Camilla* in 1844. (Author's Collection).

SHIPWRECK TREASURE

In 1945, while fishing on the Coorong, Dick Cremer and Paddy Graney found an 1837 sovereign in the gut of a butter fish, reviving memories of one of South Australia's most intriguing tales of mystery and treasure after more than 100 years.

When the *Maria* foundered near Cape Jaffa in 1840 her 25 passengers and crew set out for Encounter Bay along the sands of the Coorong, but when about 30 kilometres from the mouth of the Murray, hostile aborigines fell upon them with spears and waddies; then dismembered and ate some of the victims. Their bodies were found by searchers in several locations in the year after the massacre but to this day no one has established where they were finally buried.

The *Maria's* passengers carried about 4,000 sovereigns and early searchers followed a trail of golden coins to the scenes of the tragedies. The coins had taken the Aboriginal eyes although at that time they did not know the value of money. Apparently they used the glittering yellow things as boys use flat stones, when playing near water - they made them skim over the surface of the sea or lagoons.

Trooper's led by Police Commissioner O'Halloran relentlessly hunted down those believed responsible for the killings and the execution of natives Mongarawata and Pilgarie (some reports say Moorcangua), over the graves of some of the victims before as many natives as could be rounded up, was described by a man named Barber from the Encounter Bay whaling station:

"The major's troopers made a bungle of hanging the poor fellows. They compelled the condemned men to stand on two boxes, put the rope around their necks, and drew them tightly over an impromptu gallows. Then they kicked the boxes away and found to their horror that the men had no drop and were being slowly strangled.

The major was intensely excited and horrified and someone suggested shooting them, but this did not meet with his approval.

I went up to where he sat on his horse and told him if he would allow me I would soon hang the men.

`"Yes, yes, but be quick,"' he replied.

I got two ropes from the boat and put a rope around the body of each and we drew them up on the gallows.

When the major gave the warning (he turned his back evidently being greatly distressed) we let go and the unfortunate prisoners died instantly. After telling the blacks not to cut them down we left the place and were glad indeed, to get away."

The retribution sent a violent wave of protest around the colony and back to England, resulting in the British Government censuring the Governor of South Australia, George Gawler, despite his claims that the men had admitted their guilt and had been proved guilty by the evidence of scores of natives. For the next century tales of fiction and folklore associated with the massacre and lost treasure created an atmosphere of mystique, loneliness and danger over the Coorong to outsiders, but not to the few living there.

Most of us dream of discovering a long lost treasure sometime in our lives yet few in Australia will ever achieve that thrill. Most of the *Maria's* treasure may have been recovered but a few still cherish the hope that a fortune still awaits discovery in the shifting sands.

Some months after the hangings a member of the original search party returned to the scene of the massacres and apparently returned with a large quantity of gold and silver coins; then soon after, one of the headmen at the fishery at Encounter Bay took two bullock drays filled with blankets and other supplies into the Coorong and apparently exchanged them for gold. Nevertheless, over the years many people found coins scattered in remote parts of the Coorong and another popular, if rather vague story, tells of a man at Goolwa overturning an old tree stump near the school and finding sovereigns worth about $700.

While there might be an element of fiction in these stories of gold sovereigns, some probably still await a lucky discoverer.

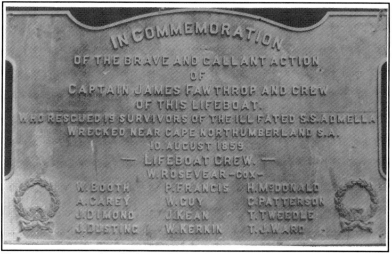

Plaque commemorating the brave deeds of the Portland lifeboat crew in the *Admella* wrecking. (Author's Collection).

The cutter *Sophia Jane* disappeared off the south eastern coast, and despite an extensive search at sea and along the coastline no trace of her was discovered. Built 1840, 15 tons, length 33ft, beam 11.4ft, depth 5.7ft.

The cutter *St. Vincent* disappeared from her moorings at Encounter Bay one evening in September and was eventually found wrecked on the beach near the mouth of the Murray River. Built 1839, 12 tons, length 32ft, beam 9.7ft, depth 5.5ft.

In November, the whaler *Isabella* encountered heavy weather which forced her ashore on the sandy beach between Rivoli Bay and Cape Northumberland. The crew cut away the masts to ensure she remained upright and all reached safety. After a short rest they travelled overland to Portland.

1845

The brig *Elizabeth Rebecca* lost her rudder in Trial Bay south of Streaky Bay on 18 April during a gale and was driven ashore, becoming a total wreck. All the crew landed safely and eventually walked overland to Port Lincoln. Built at Macquarie Harbour in 1828, the *Elizabeth Rebecca* was a brig of 99 tons, registered at Hobart Town.

The schooner *Vulcan* was driven ashore on Flinders Island on the south west coast on 22 April, while on a voyage from Adelaide to a recently established whaling station in the Recherche Archipelago. The crew built a boat using materials from their wrecked vessel and eventually reached safety. Particulars of the *Vulcan* have not been found but she may have been a vessel of around 35 tons.

The schooner *Mariner,* 46 tons, Captain Lodwick master, left Port Phillip for Adelaide late in October and had an uneventful voyage until struck by a heavy gale near Kangaroo Island. Both masts carried away, and she drifted at the mercy of the wind for several days before blowing ashore on the Coorong on 7 November.
Passengers and crew struggled ashore, only to be met by hostile natives apparently intent on plundering the cargo. Fearing for their lives, the castaways had made plans to escape along the coast when police and friendly natives arrived to rescue them and arrange transport overland to Goolwa.
Built 1839. Length 42.3ft, beam 16.6ft, depth 9.1ft.

The original Cape Jaffa lighthouse is a magnificent spectacle standing on the seafront at Kingston. Visitors can inspect its interior and climb to the lantern room, thirty-five metres above ground level. (Author's Collection).

1846

Struck by a gale off Cape Jaffa during a voyage from Adelaide to Rivoli Bay, the schooner *Victoria* capsized on the night of 9 June. As the vessel rolled over, two men were drowned, but Captain Underwood and one other member of the crew managed to launch the ship's boat

and struggle ashore. After resting they walked overland to Stirling's Station for help. Rescuers found the vessel a total loss.
Built 1837. 28 tons, length 44.6 feet; beam 14 feet; depth 6 feet.

1847

A gale drove the schooner *Alpha* on to rocks at Encounter Bay on 25 July, and she was soon a total wreck. There was no loss of life. Built in 1844 she was a wooden vessel of 35 tons.

After striking a submerged rock on 1 August the ketch *Governor Gawler* became a total wreck. Her master, Captain Underwood, a crewman and two passengers took to her dinghy and landed on Revesby Island, then were later taken to Port Lincoln. The *Governor Gawler* was a wooden vessel of 15 tons.

The cutter *William,* built on Kangaroo Island, traded between the island and Adelaide for many years. On 23 August, while entering Hog Bay in near gale conditions, she struck a reef and was lost.

1848

Early in June, during a south easterly gale, the barque *Arachne* was driven ashore and lost near Streaky Bay while sheltering with two anchors out. The crew landed safely, salvaged most of her gear, then were later taken to Adelaide on the schooner *Captain Cook* and cutter *Albatross*. Built in 1809, the *Arachne* was a vessel of 319 tons, registered at London.

The brig *Tigress,* 218 tons, was driven ashore at the mouth of the Onkarparinga River on 26 September by a violent storm. Her master, Captain Guthrie, allowed his vessel to sail too close inshore and , when an attempt was made to put her about, she missed stays and ran aground despite her anchors. The sea swept over her during the night and next morning a boat was landed and help summoned.
Unfortunately, the captain and a passenger, impatient to reach safety, were drowned when they attempted to swim ashore but as the weather moderated those left on board were landed in a whaleboat.
Captain Guthrie may have been mate on the emigrant ship *Cataraqui* when she was wrecked on King Island in 1845. He was one of only nine survivors of a disaster which cost 399 lives; his true identity has been questioned by some historians.

1849

Early in November the cutter *Gazelle* was blown ashore on the Coorong, about 8 miles north of Salt Creek. Built 1847. 17 tons, length 32ft, beam 12.7ft, depth 5.5ft.

The schooner *Young Hebe,* on her way from Adelaide to Hummock Harbour, a name now lost, somewhere near the head of

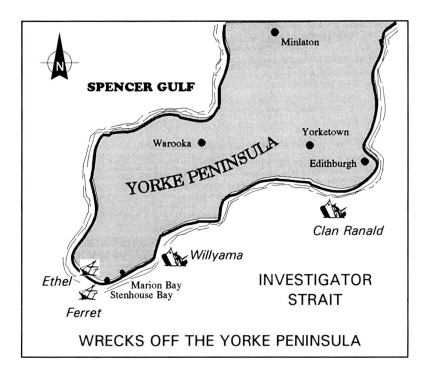

WRECKS OFF THE YORKE PENINSULA

Spencer Gulf, disappeared with her complement of ten after sailing on the 17 March. When wreckage from her was recovered off the Yorke Peninsula fears were held for her safety; then a search by the Government schooner *Yatala* located her remains among rocks about 20 miles east of Cape Spencer. No trace was ever found of her crew. The *Young Hebe* was a two masted schooner of 39 tons, built at Moulmein. She spent some time as a gunboat for the East India Company, and then as a survey vessel for the Royal Navy on the China station before being sold in 1847 at Hong Kong to Melbourne interests. At the time of her loss she was registered at Adelaide.

The cutter *Thompsons* went ashore about three miles south of Guichen Bay during a heavy gale on the night of 10 September with the loss of 22 lives. Residents realised there had been a wreck when on the next morning they found wreckage including a water cask painted a lead colour, another cask marked Calder and a third containing oil lying on a beach. The following day, part of her boat, two casks of wine, empty boxes, and her gangway rail washed in. This was followed by cargo, passenger's luggage and a woman's body.

It was thought that the *Thompsons* must have struck on one of the long reefs below the bay after having over run her distance. However, only a few pieces of the vessel came ashore; the mast from the step to the level of the deck and her pump being the only sections recognisable.

Those who lost their lives were Captain J.Wilkinson, his wife and child; Mr.and Mrs.Baxter and sister; Mr.J.Brown and servant; four seamen and a boy; also the following passengers, S.Hawkes, O.Osborn, W.Hucks, C.Causon, J.Derrick, T.Sayer, C.Cutter, T.Tacket and J.Causon, shepherds employed by the S.A.Company.

The *Thompsons* was a wooden vessel of 37 tons, built in Sydney in 1847 on dimensions of 46 x 14.3 x 7.7. She was owned by R.Venn.

The Troubridge Shoal claimed yet another victim when the ship *Sultana,* bound from London to Adelaide struck in the early hours of 28 September.   After she stranded the sea lifted her off the reef into deeper water where anchors were dropped. A boat set out for Port Adelaide for assistance and several small craft removed most of her cargo. Severe gales early in January 1850 destroyed any hopes of salvaging the ship and she was eventually broken up where she lay. Two lighters and a small cutter named *Mercy* were constructed from her timbers.   Built in 1837, the *Sultana* was a vessel of 349 tons, registered at Liverpool.

1850

The small cutter *Jane Flaxman,* 15 tons, bound for Port Lincoln with eight passengers and general cargo left Port Adelaide in fine conditions on May 2nd and was seen next day drifting towards the shore from the southwest, deserted and on her side. No sign was found of the passengers and crew and it was assumed all were washed overboard when she was pooped by a big sea. Built 1839. Length 31.7ft, beam 9.7ft, depth 4.9ft.

After an uneventful voyage from England to Adelaide, the *Grecian* was wrecked on the bar of the Port Adelaide River on 13 October. One passenger was apparently washed overboard and drowned, but the remainder and the crew reached safety on Torrens Island. Apparently the *Grecian* anchored near the lightship in a strong north westerly gale, but dragged and went ashore, where she broached with heavy seas sweeping over her. When the weather moderated her cargo was unloaded, but efforts to salvage her failed and she was sold and broken up in November 1851. Built in 1841, the *Grecian* was a wooden barque of 518 tons on dimensions of 117.5 x 29 x 19.9 feet, registered at London.

1851

After leaving Plymouth, England for Australia on 24 March 1851 with 350 passengers and a general cargo consigned to C. & F. Beck & Company of Adelaide, the emigrant ship *Marion* struck Troubridge Shoals and was lost near the western shore of the Gulf of St.Vincent on the night of 29 July.

In relatively calm conditions she grounded so easily that only a very slight shock was felt, but a decision was made to disembark all passengers while the weather was favourable. In the boats the sailors lay on their oars until daylight before attempting to land on Yorke

Peninsula. A serious accident was averted when the longboat capsized in the surf, with all passengers and crew struggling ashore, wet but unharmed.

Early next morning when the tug *Yarola* and her tender arrived at the wreck they found her standing upright and deserted on the shoal. They took some of the migrants across to Adelaide while the remainder travelled overland and a few even decided to settle in the area. It was during the journey across country to Adelaide that the sole loss of life occurred - a woman passenger was killed when a dray overturned, crushing her.

The *Marion* was a vessel of 919 tons. Her master was Captain Kissock.

THE *LADY DENISON* DISAPPEARS

The brig **Lady Denison,** 200 tons, was built at the Tasmanian convict settlement of Port Arthur in 1847 and in the following year commenced trading between Adelaide and Tasmanian ports where she became well known for several fast voyages.

On 17th April, 1850, she left Adelaide for Hobart but failed to arrive. At the time it was suspected that a number of convicts who were on board may have seized her and sailed to San Francisco to join the Californian gold rush, but her arrival there was never reported. The authenticity of several reports of her sighting at sea off the South Australian and Tasmanian coasts was never established, although a sealer claimed about three months after she disappeared that he had seen wreckage identified as coming from her scattered along the beach near Arthur River on the west coast of Tasmania. When the **Lady Denison** left Adelaide she was carrying sixteen passengers, eleven male and female convicts and three constables, in addition to her crew of seven or eight. In 1853, a policeman at Ovens in New South Wales identified a woman at an inquest as one of the convicts who had embarked on the **Lady Denison.** It is possible that if the brig had been wrecked and some of the prisoners survived, they would have preferred to be considered dead so as to regain their freedom.

On 25 April the brig *George Home* was abandoned with eight feet of water in the hold about 150 nautical miles S.S.E. of Kangaroo Island after commencing to break up. The crew spent several days in the boats before being picked up by the schooner *Elizabeth* near Cape Jervis. Built in 1809 as the 16 gun brig *Talbot* the *George Home* had been converted to a barque of 441 tons when lost.

When the brig *Flying Dutchman,* from Hobart Town to Adelaide ran ashore on the bar near the Port Adelaide River on 28 July hopes were high that she might be refloated. After her cargo was removed the sea and high winds forced her into deep water and she sank; then a gale on 16 August destroyed her. Built in 1845 she was a wooden vessel of 89 tons, registered at Hobart Town.

These few ribs half buried in the sand, and now lost forever, were believed to be
the remains of the cutter *Resource,* lost in Rivoli Bay in 1851.
(Author's Collection).

The loss of the cutter ***Resource*** in Rivoli Bay was a sad blow for
her new owner. In September 1850 she had been blown ashore in the
bay and lay there for six months before being abandoned and sold. She
was repaired and refloated, but had only been in commission for a short
time when forced ashore again nearby, becoming a total loss. Built at
Encounter Bay in 1842, she was a wooden vessel of 13 tons.

1852

The cutter ***Jane & Emma*** ran ashore on the bluff at Encounter
Bay in May and became a total wreck. No lives were lost. Built 1835.
33 tons. Length 37.9ft, beam 14.8ft, depth 7.3ft.

The schooner ***Jane Lovett,*** Captain Broadfoot, sailing between
Melbourne and Adelaide went ashore a short distance east of Cape
Northumberland on 19 September. The captain remained on board but
the crew and passengers walked to Portland.
Two shepherds, named Stephens and Crawford visited the wreck at
regular intervals to steal cargo, but, following a visit in mid October,
the captain's body was found in his bunk with his throat cut. The two
men were arrested for murder, but while awaiting trial Crawford
escaped from custody. When Stephen's learned of Crawford's escape he
made the following statement:
"I returned to the wreck with Crawford and saw the captain. While
I was in another part of the vessel I heard high words between Captain
Broadford and Crawford, which ceased on my rejoining them. After
drinking together in the cabin for some time the captain got into bed,
and while lying on his side with his face turned toward us the captain

remarked to Crawford.

"You accused me wrongfully in that matter."

Crawford then took down a razor and began strapping it idly in his hand. Broadfoot said, "What are you going to do with that razor? You are not going to cut my throat?"

Crawford replied, "I would as soon cut your throat as a sheep's, and rising up, took hold of Broadfoot's head, and with one slash nearly severed his head from his body."

Stephens was eventually taken to Adelaide, but as Crawford was never re-captured, was freed some months later.

The barque *Margaret Brock*, 245 tons, left Port Adelaide for Melbourne on 20 November, and three days later struck an offshore reef south of Guichen Bay. Although the vessel appeared only slightly damaged, the threat of a storm resulted in the passengers being landed on the beach with provisions. During the landing of provisions several of the crew narrowly escaped drowning, but after a trek northwards the party fell in with cattlemen who took them to safety. The vessel soon went to pieces.

Built at Hobart Town in 1848 on dimensions of 91.5 x 23.6 x 13.6 ft, the *Margaret Brock* was registered there when lost.

After more than 120 years beneath the sea the *Margaret Brock's* main anchor was raised in 1973 and is now at the Kingston National Trust Museum.
(Kingston National Trust).

SHIPWRECKS CHECKED CHINESE INVASION

The following year after Governor Robe visited Guichen Bay in 1846 and selected the site for a township, Robe was declared a port for immigration and overseas trade.

Early in the 1850's Chinese coolies began arriving in Victoria to reap the newly discovered golden harvest. Most were industrious, orderly and good shallow ground miners but were resented by the boozy, boisterous larrikins and adventurers frequenting the goldfields. In 1855 the Victorian Government, concerned at the growing Chinese numbers and the seething resentment building up against them, imposed a capitation tax of £10 a head on all Chinese who arrived by ship, and this forced them to disembark elsewhere outside the state boundaries and make their way overland to the goldfields of Western Victoria.

The barque *Land of Cakes* arrived at Guichen Bay on 17 January, 1857 carrying 264 Chinese and once a fee was negotiated local boats ferried the new arrivals ashore then left them to camp on the beach. In the following six months twenty seven vessels called to land Chinese, most of whom were bound for Ballarat or Bendigo. After paying up to £50 for a guide they were overlanded like cattle, but once across the border and far from their companions, were often deserted and left to fend for themselves. In any case, even the most reliable guides silently drifted away from their groups when within a few miles of their destination, for with feeling against the yellow men so high they did not wish to be involved in the incidents which often occurred when a large group of unwelcome miners arrived at the diggings.

Some of the Chinese died along the route, others dropped out and finished their days in one of the small hamlets dotting the countryside; while a few like those who stopped at Ararat discovered new goldfields. In the first six months of 1857 more than 13,000 of the invaders landed at Robe, and by the mid 1860's the flood had pushed Victoria's Chinese population past 40,000.

Under pressure from the Victorian Government, South Australia introduced a bill to restrict Chinese entry through their state, on 11 June 1857, and from this date only eight more ships arrived at Robe until the American *Maria Bradford* became the last vessel to land immigrants on 1 August 1863. Altogether, between January 1857 and August 1863, thirty five ships landed 15,382 Chinese at the port. In those years they had also delivered large quantities of tea and opium then took wool aboard to be off loaded at the major Australian ports for export overseas.

When ships discharging coolies and loading wool were lost in the bay shipowners began to favour Port MacDonnell, Kingston and Beachport. The larger ships being commissioned also found Robe's harbour too shallow. The jetty soon fell into decay and within three decades overseas trade had ceased.

1853

The barque *Duilius,* Captain Maxton was wrecked at Guichen Bay on 15 April. She was at anchor when a strong north westerly gale sprang up in the early hours and blew for several days.

At about 1.00 am on the morning of the 15th one of the anchors parted and she dragged a short distance before the wind fell away eight hours later.

Captain Maxton decided to move his vessel father off and up the bay and was raising the anchor when the cable broke. Having lost a bower anchor in coming from Melbourne and now two at Robe he had only a small stream anchor remaining, so decided to beach her.

Unfortunately, when only about a cable length off shore she touched a rock and was badly damaged. The crew eventually abandoned her but most of her equipment, stores and cargo of wool, the first to be loaded at Guichen Bay for London were saved.

Built in 1840, the *Duilus* was a wooden, three masted barque of 327 tons.

The schooner *Witness,* 121 tons, Captain McKenzie, on a voyage from Adelaide to Melbourne, was totally wrecked on Cape Northumberland on the night of 1 May. The night was dark with light drizzling rain, and the ship was among the breakers before the crew realised their danger.

The high seas washed the schooner right over the reef otherwise all hands would have been lost, but they remained on board until daylight when a boat was launched and some of the crew landed. Some time later thirty casks of brandy and other goods washed ashore and were salvaged.

On 29 June the 11 ton cutter *Midge* was driven on to rocks near Cape Willoughby lighthouse while trading between Port Adelaide and Encounter Bay, and became a total wreck.

S.S.Osmanli was lost off Kangaroo island on the night of 25 November owing principally to a mistake of twenty-five miles in the estimate of her position and mistaking the land at night during a voyage from Melbourne to Adelaide.

All the crew and passengers, numbering 83, landed safely by boat and remained on shore while some of the crew returned to the wreck for food and other necessities. Help eventually arrived from Adelaide but the steamer soon became a total loss despite salvage attempts.

Built in 1846, 403 tons. Length 180ft, beam 23.7ft.

The schooner *Emu,* Captain Evans and crew of three, left Port Elliot for Adelaide with a cargo of 164 bags of wheat, but two days later returned and anchored a short distance off shore when bad weather threatened.

The obelisk on Cape Dombey at Robe, built of stone in 1855 as a guide to shipping entering Guichen Bay. Originally all white, it was painted in alternate red and white bands in 1862 to make it more easily seen from out at sea. For some years rocket gear was stored in its base.   (Author's Collection).

Next morning she was missing from her anchorage and a search along the beach uncovered her hull broken in halves and driven up into the sand. The fore section was keel upwards but all the cargo had disappeared and numerous pieces of wreckage were floating in the surf. From the position in which the wreck was found and the distance over which it extended, local authorities considered she must have broken up on Frenchman's Rock, about a quarter of a mile from the shore and about half a mile from where she was moored.

The only articles saved from the wreck were the log book, account book, captain's hat, cabin table, boat, a few spars, ropes and hatches. The bodies of the drowned sailors were never recovered.

Built 1847. 21 tons. Length 39 ft, beam 11.5 ft, depth 5.9 ft.

1854

Strong currents forced the brig *Charles Carter* off course as she attempted to enter the Gulf of St.Vincent at the conclusion of her voyage from Mauritius to Adelaide, and she ran ashore on Troubridge Shoal near the wrecks of the *Sultana* and *Marion*, in the early hours of 23 February. Salvage attempts were progressing favourably until bad weather early in March almost destroyed her. Built in 1833, the *Charles Carter* was a wooden vessel of 175 tons.

The figurehead of the barque *Mozambique* is displayed on a building in Goolwa. The barque was driven ashore on the nearby Coorong by heavy seas in 1854. (Author's Collection).

The *Mozambique* left London for Melbourne with 24 passengers and a crew of 22, but after an uneventful voyage ran into heavy seas off the Coorong and was driven ashore. When a local resident, William Low, discovered the wreck, all had reached safety but were suffering from exposure and exhaustion. He immediately gave them food and water before taking them in his boat to Goolwa where they received every attention. One passenger later died from his privations. The *Mozambique* was a wooden barque of 402 tons, built in 1832.

The sloop *O.G.* was lost in Yankallila Bay in May when forced ashore after her anchor dragged. Built 1840, 9 tons. Length 28 ft, beam 10.5ft, depth 4.5ft.

A gale forced the cutter *Industry* ashore at Yankalilla on 18 August after she had been anchored offshore in high seas for several hours. Her master and crew left her in a boat which capsized in the surf, forcing them to swim for their lives. The cutter's cable soon parted, and she drove ashore where she was hauled up on the beach pending efforts to refloat her. Apparently this was not successful. Built 1852, of 8 tons. Length 26.5 ft, beam 7.7 ft, depth 5 ft.

The *Nene Valley,* Captain R.C.Baldwin, inward bound from London to Portland, was wrecked close to Cape Northumberland on the night of 19 October. On the one hundred and fiftieth day out, the captain left the deck at 10.00pm, but was called out shortly before midnight by the Second Mate. He believed his ship too far to the east so immediately ordered the helmsman to "luff" to the wind while he went below for his glasses. Before he returned, the ship had stuck, sending her masts crashing over the side. A boat was launched, and a rope fastened to the shore, but the next boat capsized, although its occupants reached safety. After all had landed, a boat containing the First and Second Mates, carpenter and three crewmen returned to the wreck to cut away the mast. Their task completed, they were rejoining their comrades when their boat overturned drowning the Second Mate and the three seamen.

The captain, passengers and other survivors walked thirty miles to the mouth of the Glenelg River, where horses were obtained and the captain rode to Portland to report the disaster. The *Nene Valley* was a wooden barque of 333 tons.

1855

On the night of 30 January, the schooner *Sanspariel,* on a voyage from Melbourne to Adelaide with cargo and mails, ran on to a reef extending south-east from Cape Jervis and became a total wreck. No lives were lost.

A gale parted the anchor cable of the cutter *Joseph Lee Archer* as she lay at anchor in Guichen Bay and she drove onto rocks where she became a total wreck. Captain Buckmater and his crew reached safety. Built 1848 of 35 tons. Length 44.6 ft, beam 13.5 ft, depth 7.4ft.

The barque *Iron Age,* 361 tons, Captain Brown, bound from Liverpool to Portland with a general cargo was forced ashore near Cape Banks on the night of 15 February. Running before the wind she ploughed across a reef and remained intact long enough to enable the crew to reach safety. At the time, Captain Brown believed the ship was forty miles off shore, and was about to alter course when she struck.

At the inquiry into the wreck, Captain Brown stated that he believed a strong current and deviation in the compasses were responsible for the loss of the barque.

Skindivers who visit her remains recover bricks from her cargo and a few fittings of value, although most of her timbers have disappeared.

Built at Stockton, England in 1854, and registered at London, the *Iron Age* was an iron barque.

At the conclusion of an uneventful voyage out from Liverpool with nearly 300 Irish emigrants, among whom were 130 single girls, the ship *Nashwauk* went ashore about two miles south of the mouth of the Onkaparinga River on 12 May, when a light on shore was mistaken for the lightship. Passengers and mails were landed next morning shortly before the weather changed. Heavy seas swept in over the ship which was lying in about two fathoms under high cliffs, with twelve feet of water in the holds. The steamers *Melbourne* and *Yatala* anchored off the wreck and some passengers were eventually embarked and taken up to Adelaide. Others preferred to walk overland to the town, while a few took jobs in the district.

A heavy gale eventually destroyed the ship, with the masts collapsing and ripping open the hull, allowing the cargo to spill out and be swept away, strewing the beach with wreckage for miles. At a sale held on the beach the hull brought £70 while sundry items totalled about £600.

Blaming the captain for her loss, a Court of Inquiry found that he failed to chart the vessel's position and course on the night before the wreck.

The *Nashwauk* was a vessel of 765 tons commanded by Captain MacIntyre.

1856

The ship *Varoon,* 598 tons, Captain Robertson, master, bound from Manilla to Sydney with a cargo of sugar, cigars, tobacco and rope, was wrecked about twenty miles west of Cape Northumberland late in January.

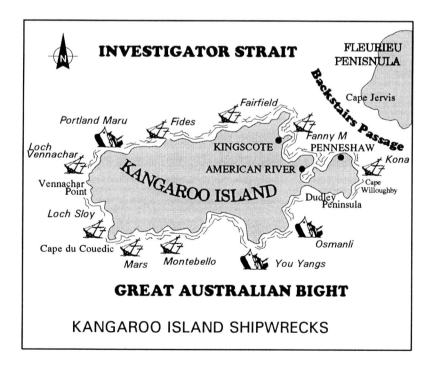

KANGAROO ISLAND SHIPWRECKS

The wreck was only discovered after a number of bodies were found on the beach near Cape Bridgewater in Victoria. The remains of one, lashed to part of the rigging appeared from the clothing to have been the captain, but most of the other bodies appeared to be those of Lascar seamen.

The mails were found after a tedious search along the coast, during which a mounted policeman's horse stumbled over a tin box which contained the ship's papers. Seventy cases of cigars and many sugar bags later washed ashore, but the largest pieces of wreckage were the mast and yards which came ashore at Cape Bridgewater.

The *Varoon* was built in 1853 and registered at Aberdeen.

The cutter *Maid Of The Mill* left Adelaide for Willunga on 27 February with a cargo of palings, flour and sundries. A gale forced her ashore near Onkarparinga where she became a total wreck.

This was a most disasterous year for Port Elliot when no less than four vessels were lost in the bay, raising doubts concerning its future as a port.

Port Elliot, the scene of several disasterous wrecks, photographed sometime after 1890. (Author's Collection).

The schooner *Commodore,* a vessel of 61 tons arrived from Adelaide on February 1 and anchored close to Rocky Point. Later in the day a strong wind sprang up and at about midnight the schooner parted her anchor and blew onto the rocks where she soon became a total wreck. Most of the cargo was lost; only a few sails and fittings being salvaged. Commodore Point received its name from this wreck.

Five months later, on the morning of July 10th, the brigantine *Josephine L'Oizeau* arrived from Adelaide with 120 tons of cargo valued at about £3000 and many passengers expecting to board the paddle steamer *Albury* at Goolwa and proceed up the Murray River. Late in the afternoon the wind freshened from the south and soon reached gale force. At about ten in the evening the schooner's anchor parted and she went ashore. Her master, Captain Mennie and the Harbour Master organised rescue operations immediately the vessel struck and thirteen women and children were quickly taken to safety. The crew spent the next few days salvaging all that remained but most of the flour in the cargo was so badly damaged by water it was abandoned.

The cutter *Lapwing* was the next vessel lost when strong easterly gales blew two vessels ashore early in September. The *Lapwing* and the schooner *Swordfish* were forced ashore despite the frantic efforts of their crews and the Harbour Master. Two men who returned to the *Lapwing* for personal effects after she had been abandoned were drowned.

The strength of the gales may be gauged from the report that the *Swordfish* let out four anchors and was strongly connected to the harbour moorings, yet these did not hold her. The *Lapwing* lay broadside on to the surf and within a few days had gone to pieces, but the *Swordfish* lying stern on to the beach exactly where the *Josephine L'Oizeau* was lost, was refloated a few days later suffering only minor damage.

The final wreck for the year saw the brig *Harry,* loaded with 412 bales of wool and 1642 bags of lead ore go ashore near Commodore Point. She was being taken by the Harbour Master and Pilot from the river to the outer moorings when the wind dropped and she drifted on to the point. Her anchor was let out but it would not hold, while ropes passed around nearby rocks were quickly cut to pieces. As the tide rose the *Harry* began to bump heavily forcing the crew to cut away the foremast to lighten and steady her before the cargo was unloaded.

Details of ships lost at Port Elliot:
Commodore. Wooden schooner, 61 tons, owned by J.Coleman.
Josephine L'Oizeau, brigantine of 94 tons, built in 1841 and registered in Port Adelaide.
Lapwing. Cutter of 62 tons, built in 1808.
Harry, brig of 199 tons, built in 1842 and registered at Port Adelaide.

The barge *Schnieder* sank at Port Elliot.

The schooner *Grenada* which stranded at Port Willunga on 21 June was refloated only to go ashore again a few days later and become a total wreck. She lay broadside on to the beach with no hope of refloating, so was dismantled where she lay. The *Grenada* was a brig of 156 tons, registered at Liverpool.

The barge *Goulburn* foundered between Cape Jervis and Kangaroo Island while under tow.

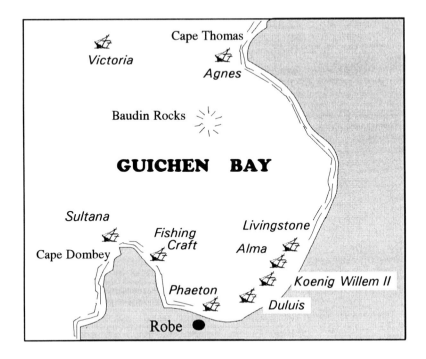

1857

This was Robe's worst year for shipwrecks.

The American ship **Phaeton** arrived from Hong Kong on the morning of 1 February with a general cargo and 260 Chinese. At about 7 a.m. she sighted the obelisk on Cape Dombey about eight miles away and after tacking off shore stood into the bay. When in about five fathoms the helm was put down but she missed stays. The head sheets were hauled aft and she gathered way once again, only to miss stays a second time.

With all sails aback, an anchor was dropped; then a kedge was run out until taut. As the wind began on increase the sails were then clewed and furled and a stream anchor was also dropped. Suddenly, the ship commenced to strike heavily aft and within ten minutes had nine feet of water in the hold. She was afloat up forward with more than four fathoms under the bow and her head right in shore, but as she was filling fast the boats were got out and the royal and top gallant yards sent down.

The crew also set to making a raft to land the passengers as the surf was considered too heavy for the boats. By this time the ship had settled fast on the port side and there was more than three feet of water in the between decks.

The wind moderated as evening approached and by early next morning all the passengers had been landed. Some of the boats had also been upset in the surf without any casualties. Following a survey a few days later the entire vessel and most of her cargo were condemned. Only 200 chests of tea were saved but most of the ship's fittings and gear were recovered.

The *Phaeton*, 1032 tons was a new ship on only her second voyage. Captain Morrison, her master, was accompanied on this voyage by his wife and family.

On 27 April the ship *Sultana,* with a general cargo and more Chinese passengers from Hong Kong struck on Cape Dombey at the entrance to Guichen Bay and began taking water. The pumps were manned but as the water continued to gain she was run ashore to allow all to land safely. The ship was soon a total wreck.

Later, her acting master complained that there was no pilot to the port and at the time his ship struck the weather was so thick he could not locate any identifying points.

On 16 May the wreck was sold as she lay on the beach with her cargo, all fitting and rigging. Here, taken from the South Australian Register is a list of the cargo she carried: 80 tons Bally Rice, 150 watercasks, each of 200 gallons, 10 packets of teaseed oil in tins and boxes, 43 cases of clothing, 15 baskets of ginger, 50 baskets of potatoes, 20 packets of Chinese medicine, 2 iron water tanks.

The *Sultana* was a vessel of 588 tons. When lost she was under the command of the mate, the captain having died on the passage out.

This cannon on the flagstaff mound at Robe is believed to have come from the wreck of the Dutch barque *Koning Willem de Tweede (Koenig Willem II)*, wrecked in 1857. Some claim it is from the barque *Duiluis*, wrecked at Robe in 1853. (Author's Collection).

Sixteen lives were lost when the Dutch barque *Koenig Willem II* from Hong Kong was lost at Guichen Bay on 30 June after all her Chinese passengers had been safely landed. The ship had been ready to sail for several days but bad weather had prevented her continuing her voyage. On the morning she was lost the strong wind had increased to a gale from the south west.

Although all the upper spars and fittings had been sent down she drifted from her anchorage until about noon when the force of the gale tore the windlass out of the ship, forcing the master to raise sail in an attempt to beach her. She finally grounded to the east of Robe on Long Beach and became a total wreck immediately as terrific seas swept over her endangering the lives of all on board. News of the wreck spread rapidly and all the men in the employ of Messrs Omerod hurried to the scene where they were joined by soldiers and police.

Soon after the barque struck a boat was launched containing the mate and crew, with the exception of the captain who was left stranded on the wreck when the boat's painter broke. The boat had proceeded only a short distance when it broached, filled quickly, leaving the occupants struggling for their lives in the breakers. Of the twenty-five who left the ship, nine, including the mate were dragged ashore more dead than alive. Those on shore now turned their efforts to the rescue of the master, clinging to the vessel's stern. He pointed frantically to the boats lying on the beach but they were damaged and useless. Even had they been seaworthy it would have been impossible to attempt a rescue in the conditions.

After sunset most of those at the scene returned home, leaving a few on the beach in case the ship broke up during the night. John Omerod promised £50 to any boat's crew if they succeeded in rescuing the captain while an aboriginal from Encounter Bay volunteered to swim out if he was paid a small reward. While these plans were being discussed the wind shifted slightly and this allowed the captain to drift a cask to shore with a rope attached, after which the men on the beach were able to safely draw him through the surf.

For the next few days wreckage and bodies washed ashore. The human remains were in such a decomposed state that it was thought better to bury them on the spot. Although police maintained a close watch on the beach, plunderers stole cargo, fittings, and also broke open chests belonging to the unfortunate seamen as they washed ashore.

On 11 July the remains of the *Koenig Willem II* were purchased by J.Chambers of Robe for £225. He dismantled most of the wreck but left two cannon from her lying wedged between rocks. They were later salvaged and placed on the Flagstaff Hill in Royal Circus. Vandals destroyed one and the second was removed to a private home where it remained for many years before being returned to Flagstaff Hill.

The *Koenig Willem II* was a vessel of 800 tons under the command of Captain Giezen.

The brig *Ida* with 30 tons of copper ore from Port Wakefield went ashore at Port Willunga on 15 January, after snapping her Government moorings and dragging an anchor in near gale conditions. Next morning she lay a total wreck with her back broken and full of water.

CARPENTER ROCKS

Although Grant had named Cape Banks, which overlooks the rocks, on 3 December 1800, he had not approached close to shore, and so missed sighting the dangerous reef.

Carpenter Rocks are two black rocks projecting above high water about one and a half miles north west of the Cape, and were named by Peron, zoologist with the Baudin expedition, who said the rocks were indented like the teeth of a carpenter's saw.

Flinders, in his "Voyage to Terra Australis" published in 1814, describes his encounter with the rocks thus: *"At nine o'clock we bore away southward, keeping at the distance of two or three miles from the shore. It was the same kind of hummock-topped bank as before described; but a ridge of moderately high hills, terminated to the southward by a bluff, was visible over it; three or four leagues inland; and there was a reef of rocks lying in front of the shore.*

"At noon, two large rocks were seen at the southern end of the reef, and are those called by the French "The Carpenters". They lie one or two miles from a sandy projection named by them Cape Boufflers; but here a prior title to discovery interferes. "

Tourists will have little trouble reaching a point where the reef may be easily seen. A good bitumen road runs from Mount Gambier to the fishing village of Carpenter Rocks, and from there a gravel road runs through the sandhills to the entrance gate of the lighthouse reserve on Cape Banks. Leave the car in the parking area at the entrance and climb the sandhills overlooking the beach. The reef is always visible. Approaching from the western side, turn off the highway and drive to Carpenter Rocks via Tantanoola.

The *Manhou* arrived in St Vincent's Gulf on 15 August, 114 days out from Hong Kong on her way to Guichen Bay with 338 Chinese. While anchored off Semaphore taking on additional food and water a gale forced her to head for Port Adelaide. Unfortunately she ran on to a reef off Port Willunga and after being refloated on the 21st was put up for auction on 11 January 1858, following extensive repairs. Her new owners found she needed more repairs and so she was broken up.

The brigantine *Maid of the Valley*, 128 tons was driven ashore at Port Willunga on 13 November and was evidently not worth repairing.

The brig *Halcyon* was wrecked about six mile south from the mouth of the Murray River. In charge of Captain Patterson, she was sailing to Port Elliot, but when driven close to the Murray beach, the masts were cut away and two anchors let go in a desperate attempt to save her. When the anchors finally parted, a jury sail was rigged and the vessel ran ashore. A boat was lowered but it capsized in the surf, forcing the occupants to return to the ship. Later the wind moderated and all reached safety. Built in 1848, the *Halcyon* was a wooden vessel of 192 tons, measuring 97.3ft x 21.5ef x 13.4 ft.

1858

The schooner *Rose* disappeared between Black Point on the Yorke Peninsula and Adelaide in about mid-April. She was a vessel of 40 tons, built in 1853.

The cutter *Venture* was lost at Snapper Point, Kangaroo Island, on 14 September.

1859

The brigantine *Nora Criena*, commanded by Captain Lowe, left Adelaide for Melbourne via Guichen Bay on 21 December 1858. On 1 January 1859 a few hours after leaving Guichen Bay, she struck what appeared to be a shoal, and when freed filled rapidly and sank in deep water within thirty-five minutes. Passengers and crew took to the boats and returned safely to Robe.

The remains of the ship were later sold for a mere £5. Built in 1834, 172 tons, she was registered in Melbourne. Measurements 82.6 x 20.4 x 14.2 ft.

During a gale, the cutter *Mary,* bound for Yankililla and Port Willunga, was wrecked off Port Willunga on 11 February. Her crew of four escaped drowning, but only a few stores were recovered. Built in 1856, 17 tons. Length 38ft, beam 12.4ft, depth 6.3ft.

Crossing the bar at the mouth of the Murray River where it enters the sea near Goolwa was always a risky business, but buoys were placed to mark the channel which was navigable in calm weather. The paddle steamer *Melbourne* which crossed the bar every fortnight, was clearing the river on 16 November when a steam pipe burst, leaving her without power.

She drifted on to the end of Sir Richard Peninsula, where an anchor was dropped to steady her in the swell. However, she rolled on to it and was holed, forcing the crew to use the last remaining steam to take her upstream where she might have been saved.

However she soon sank and eventually became a total wreck, although some of her cargo of 114 bales of wool was recovered.

The *Melbourne* was built for the Melbourne-Geelong trade, and after being bought by Cadell for use on the Murray River also spent some time operating between Port Adelaide and Goolwa.

In 1854 while sailing between Port Elliot and Adelaide, she collided with *S.S.Champion* in Backstairs Passage and was badly damaged.

She was a paddle steamer of 153 tons on dimensions of 134.5ft x 17ft x 8.3ft. Her master when lost was Captain Barber.

Early in 1859 the barque *Favourite* was driven ashore at Antechamber Bay, Kangaroo Island while sheltering from a gale, when on her way from Newcastle to Adelaide with coal.

She was sold, refloated, then converted into a coal hulk at Port Adelaide.

The schooner *Waitemata* left Port Adelaide for Western Australian ports on 27 April with three passengers and a general cargo. A westerly gale forced her to shelter at Kingscote and American River, Kangaroo Island, for several days before she set a course for St.Peter's Island near Ceduna, where water provisions were replenished. Soon after leaving she began to leak badly so was run ashore on St Francis Island on 20 May.

Passengers and crew landed safely and later a boat was sent across to St.Peter's Island to ask for assistance. After many weeks, the *Yatala* called and took them aboard. Most of the cargo was salvaged before the vessel went to pieces.

The *Waitemata* was a wooden schooner of 59 tons built at Auckland, New Zealand in 1852 on dimensions of 62.5ft x 18ft x 7.4ft. Her master was Captain Harris.

Becalmed when off Cape Borda, Kangaroo Island during the final hours of a voyage from London to Adelaide with a general cargo, the barque *Fides* eventually drifted ashore a few miles to the east on the morning of 22 May.

Swept by heavy seas soon after striking she broke up rapidly and only six of her crew of fifteen reached the shore. All had been injured when raging seas threw them against rocks, but after resting they set out for the Cape Borda lighthouse which was reached after battling for two days through thick scrub.

The lightkeepers returned to the wreck with the survivors a few days later, but only one or two bodies were recovered and buried. Very little cargo remained undamaged. After resting for a few days the crew left by lifeboat for Port Adelaide, and after a miserable voyage eventually reached their destination about a fortnight after the wreck.

The schooner *Alexander* proceeded to the wreck and recovered some cargo before returning to Adelaide on 6 July. The *Fides* was a vessel of 387 tons. Her master was Captain F. Aspland.

The brigantine *Flying Fish,* loaded with twenty bales of wool for Melbourne broke away from her moorings at Port Elliot during a heavy gale on 3 December and drove ashore where she quickly went to pieces.

The nine members of the crew reached safety along a line after drifting a buoy with a light line attached ashore where a youth named Dent showed great courage by wading out into the huge breakers and bringing it ashore. Soon after the crew left the ship, the sea threw her high onto the beach breaking her back.

Once again the weakness of the moorings and the unfinished state of the breakwater came under strong criticism. Built at Hobart Town in 1843, the *Flying Fish* was a wooden vessel of 111 tons, measuring 83.4 x 18.9 x 10 feet.

1861

The cutter *Henry and Mary* left Kangaroo Island for Adelaide but when off Port Willunga, became uncontrollable in heavy seas. An anchor was dropped but this soon dragged and she struck a reef which quickly destroyed her. The master, his wife, two seamen and a child remained on the wreck until rescued. Built in 1852, 16 tons. Length 38.8ft, beam 12 ft, depth 5.7ft.

The Government moorings at Port MacDonnell came under strong criticism after strong gales had blown two vessels ashore on 17th and 18th April.

Several vessels were anchored in MacDonnenell Bay when the wind suddenly freshened from the north, then veered around quickly to blow a gale from the south west.

All vessels put out more anchors but the schooner *Adelaide* began to pitch and roll in an alarming manner as she gradually dragged into the breakers. By evening she was lying broadside to the surf with her back broken, full of water. The gale increased during the night, driving the schooner *Bandicoot* ashore next day near the wreck of the *Jane Lovett*. No lives were lost.

The *Bandicoot* was built in 1838, 55 tons. Length 51ft:, beam 14.6ft., depth 9.7ft. The *Adelaide* was built in 1831, of 78 tons, registered in Melbourne.

On 24 May, during a gale, the barque *Miami* blew ashore from her anchorage in MacDonnell Bay and broke her back. The crew struggled ashore and a short time later her hull washed up on to the beach where a public auction of the remains and cargo was held. The hull, rigging and fittings along with 500 bags of flour and 150 bags of wheat were sold for £651/1/6. Now, the sea occasionally washes the sand away to expose two rows of water-washed timbers.

The *Miami* was a three masted barque of 229 tons, built in 1848 on dimensions of 91.2 x 23.7 x 13.6 feet. Registered in Sydney.

About mid October, the brig, *John Omerod,* Captain Sevior, left Adelaide for Sydney with a cargo of flour. When about fifty miles off Cape Northumberland she was forced on to her beam ends by a sudden squall, submerging the port cabins and drowning the steward. The crew clung to the ship's rails fearing she would capsize as giant waves swept over her washing away the mate and several of the crew before the mainmast was cut away, enabling her to slowly return to an even keel.

Through the night the vessel drifted helplessly before the gale, and at dawn only the captain and two seamen remained. Late afternoon the brig drifted close to Cape Northumberland and eventually the three men were rescued by the pilot boat which was visiting the lighthouse.

The derelict continued to drift and was boarded again near Cape Douglas when the body of the drowned steward and personal effects were recovered. Some time later the wreck washed ashore about thirty miles west of Portland. Built in 1826, the *John Omerod* was a vessel of 187 tons measuring 87.6 x 22.3 x 15 ft. Registered in Sydney.

The schooner *Emu* was engaged to carry piles from Port MacDonnell to Lacepede Bay, and she left in December, but disappeared without trace. Fourteen years later wreckage was discovered near the southern end of Rivoli Bay and close examination identified it as part of the *Emu*. Built in 1851, of 36 tons. Length 52.4ft, beam 15.5ft, depth 7.1ft.

Heavy gales battered the south east coast in mid December destroying two more vessels in Guichen Bay. The *Alma* was in ballast preparing to load wool and the *Livingstone* was already loaded with wool and copper when the gale swept in from the north west during the night. The *Alma* had been riding to one anchor but a second was let go. However, in the early hours the starboard cable parted so the topgallants were struck and preparations made to let a third anchor out. Despite these precautions the ship began to drag dangerously and although the crew worked feverishly to cut away the masts she eventually ran aground on the rocks.

A dance was being held at the Caledonian Inn at the time and the master of the *Alma* who was attending could not return to his ship, so was forced to remain on shore and watch his vessel being battered to pieces. The rocket crew also hurried to the beach where the coxswain of the lifeboat, a man named Fergus Fullerton, fired the first rocket with a line attached towards the wreck. Being elevated too high, the wind carried it away and it fell a few yards beyond the stern. The elevation was lowered but the second also missed its mark. Fortunately, the third went across the bowsprit, the end of the line was made fast on board, a heavy hawser was dragged out and then secured at both ends. A lifeboat was rigged to this and Fullerton hauled himself out to the wreck to explain how it could be used. When returning to the shore he was hurled against rocks and suffered painful injuries.

Within an hour all twenty-four members of the crew were ashore, but during the night the *Alma* went to pieces and next morning only portion of the bow remained.

The *Alma* was a barque of 516 tons from London. Her master was Captain Ogelvie.

The *Livingstone* went ashore on the Long Beach next day, not far from the remains of the *Alma*. When the gale first struck she lay with two anchors out but even though her foremast was cut away she dragged slowly towards the rocks. In her case the lifeboat was able to rescue the crew before she went ashore where she hogged in ten feet of water at high tide. All her fittings were removed and eventually most of the cargo recovered. The wool was washed and at a sale held on the cliffs at the back of the Newtown Arms, realised £40,000.

The *Livingstone* was a barque of 531, tons, also from London. Her master was Captain J. Prynn.

1862

The small schooner *Walrus,* 88 tons, sailed from Port MacDonnell on 21 February and is believed to have foundered at sea.

1863

The steamer **Marion** went ashore near Cape Spencer in foggy conditions on 11 July 1862. By 10.00am as the tide rose she began to break up. Within a few hours her masts and funnel disappeared, and she broke amidships as the stern settled in deep water. Passengers and crew numbering about fifty were landed safely and later taken to Port Adelaide by the *S.S.Lubra*. The **Marion** was a vessel of 197 tons, built in 1854.

In calm conditions, the two-masted schooner **Agenora** drifted ashore at Port Willunga on 14 January where she eventually broke up. Built in 1855, of 53 tons. Length 55.9ft, beam 19ft, depth 7.8ft.

Bound from Adelaide to Yankalilla, the cutter **Breeze** was forced south by a gale and eventually wrecked near American River, Kangaroo Island, on 5 July. Built in 1848, of 18 tons. Length 33.9 ft, beam 9.4ft, depth 5.9ft.

1864

The brig **Freak** left Port Adelaide for Sydney on 27 March with a cargo of flour, bran, hay, wheat and apples, but ran ashore on Cape Jervis and became a total wreck. No lives were lost.

A few months later the brigantine **Vanguish** suffered a similar mishap after leaving Adelaide for Melbourne on 4 December with a cargo of wheat, barley, pollard and bones. At midnight, in foggy weather she ran ashore on Cape Jervis and filled rapidly. There was no loss of life and most of her cargo was salvaged, although damaged by water.
Built in 1846, the **Vanguish** was a wooden vessel of 128 tons. Her master was Captain Leddra.

The build up of shipping waiting to load at Port Elliot and the scandalous rate of progress in the construction of the tramway were blamed by many as the major cause of the loss of the schooner *Athol* from Newcastle.
After waiting more than a fortnight to load about 500 bags of wheat and flour, rough weather rolled in from the south forcing all vessels at anchor to strengthen their moorings. The rocket gear was set up in readiness by the Harbour Master who then visited three vessels; the *Athol*, *Eliza Corry,* and *Alexandra* riding at the outer moorings, and assisted them in their preparations to ride out the gales.
However, during the storm, the deeply-laden *Athol* drifted into shallow water and eventually grounded on rocks near where the *Commodore* had been lost eight years earlier. After attempts to save her had failed, her master ordered the foremast cut away to lighten her while boats and ropes fastened to the shore were used to land the crew, portion of the cargo and sails.
Several rendering assistance narrowly escaped death when the Harbour Master's boat capsized alongside the wreck, but those on shore

rushed into the surf and saved them from being swept on to the rocks.

The *Athol* was a vessel of 215 tons, built in 1853 and registered in Newcastle.

1865

The schooner *Agnes,* Captain Taylor, bound from Yankalilla to Melbourne with wheat was wrecked on Cape Jaffa Reef on the night of 13 March. Heavy winds and seas battered her after she passed Cape Willoughby, and she was eventually driven on to the reef and swept by high seas. One man was washed overboard soon after she struck and others were swept from the rigging later, leaving only the master and a seaman named Backer clinging to the schooner as she commenced to break up.

Backer improvised a raft, drifted ashore then walked overland to Robe for help. Rescuers found wreckage drifting over a wide area and after a short search recovered the captain's body.

Built in Scotland in 1840, the *Agnes* was registered in Melbourne.

The barque *San Miquel* left Port Adelaide on 6 May with a mixed cargo, heading toward Wallaroo to top up ore for Swansea, Wales, but at about 4.00am on the 7th ran on to Tipara Reef. The tug *Eleanor* from Adelaide tried unsuccessfully to free her, and then a heavy gale removed hopes of salvage. Built in 1864, the *San Miquel* was an iron vessel of 535 tons, registered at Liverpool.

The barque *Troas* ran ashore near the northern end of Lake Bonney on 14 May, and soon broke up. No lives were lost. She was bound for Foochow, China, in ballast, and carried only forty cases of jam. Apparently the mud ballast she loaded in Adelaide became wet when the vessel leaked, then shifted in heavy seas making her almost unmanageable. For several days she drifted aimlessly before striking a reef a short distance offshore.
Heavy surf soon carried away the masts and she was eventually lifted over the reef into shallow water, enabling all hands to reach shore along a rope.

Captain Desborough told a Marine Court Inquiry in Adelaide that if stone or other proper ballast had been carried, the wreck would not have occurred. He was exonerated from all blame.

Built in 1857 at Sunderland, and registered there, the *Troas* was a wooden vessel of 663 tons, measuring 152 x 31 x 20.5 ft.

The government cutter *Blanche* was moored near the jetty at Port Wallaroo on the night of 25 July when she dragged her anchor during a gale, went ashore, and was soon battered beyond repair by the heavy surf. One of the crew donned a lifebelt, took a line in his hands, jumped overboard and scrambled ashore. The line was fastened to a pile of an old jetty, enabling the remaining two seamen on board to reach safety. The *Blanche* was a vessel of 34 tons. Her master was Captain Graham.

LIFEBOATS AND ROCKET CREWS

The Port MacDonnell lifeboat *Undaunted* at practice in 1909. It was the third boat stationed there until withdrawn in 1930; then wrecked off nearby Green Point in 1951 after use for air and sea rescue operations during World War 2. (Les Hill).

The south eastern coastline of South Australia exacted a high toll in ships and human life. To the end of 1879 at least 48 vessels had been lost there including the *Admella* (89 lives) and *Geltwood* (31 lives) .

The first lifeboat in South Australia, the *Lady Daly,* was launched in 1867 for use at Adelaide replacing a whaleboat named *Rescue* which had served the growing port since 1861. Port MacDonnell's first boat, probably similar to the one at Adelaide went into service in 1860 under the command of Ben Germein the famous lighthouse keeper, and it was replaced by the lifeboat *Percy* in 1861. The last boat at Port MacDonnell arrived in 1908 and remained until 1930 .

The boat used at Robe in the early days was probably a converted whaleboat, and Beachport which came into being in 1878 after demands for a safe port grew, also had an ordinary rowing boat under the control of the Harbour Master. A headstone in the Robe cemetery also recalls a lifeboat accident near there on 23 June, 1883 when the boat *Lady Jervis* overturned in the surf while at practice, drowning two members of the crew.

Following the wreck of the *Star of Greece* in July 1888, the lifeboat service was placed under the control of the South Australian Colonial Navy, and the only surviving boat from this era is the unique water jet propelled *City of Adelaide* which arrived at Adelaide from England in 1896 . Built of galvanised steel, she was 52 feet long, and had a beam of 16 feet, with a total capacity of 80 persons.

The Port MacDonnell lifeboat *Percy* rescues survivors from the wreck of the coal barque *Agnes* shortly before it broke up on 18 July, 1876.
(Author's Collection).

It was transferred to Beachport in 1896, but its propulsion system suffered some problems during its career, and while it did not attend a shipwreck it stood by several ships in distress and helped save many lives.

In 1905, Port Victor (Victor Harbour), received the *Lady Daly* from Adelaide, and it and the stations at Beachport and Port MacDonnell continued to function until 30 June 1931 when they and fifteen rocket stations were abolished.

The *City of Adelaide* has been declared an Historic Shipwreck under the South Australian Act, 1981, and is now on display at Port Lincoln. Most rocket gear was stored at lighthouses or police stations along the coast, but Robe kept theirs in the obelisk on Cape Dombey. Carts were used to haul the gear, and the crew usually contained between 9 and 15 men. Stations were established at Port Lincoln, Cape Borda, Cape du Couedic, Cuttle Fish Bay, Kingscote, Port Adelaide, Glenelg, Aldinga, Normanville, Port Victor, Cape Dombey, Kingston, Beachport and Port MacDonnell. All were disbanded in 1931.

1866

The schooner *Omeo* disappeared off the Yorke Peninsula late in July. A companion slide, two hatches, a boom, part of a boat and a galley identified as belonging to her were picked up off Corney Point. She was a two-masted wooden schooner of 40 tons, built at Melbourne in 1854 on dimensions of 44.3ft x 15.3ft x 6.6ft. Captain Wills was her master.

The cutter *Fire Fly* arrived at Anxious Bay from Flinders Island on 20 October with seventy bales of wool, and anchored in the face of a strong north westerly gale. Two days later both anchors parted and she went ashore where she broke in two. Forty-eight of her wool bales were washed ashore and eventually recovered. Built at Port Adelaide in 1855, the *Fire Fly* was a cutter of 51 tons on dimensions of 49.3 x 14.3 x 9.5ft. After alterations in 1861 she was of 33 tons on dimensions of 52 x 15.2 x 8.4ft. When lost she was insured for £200. Her master was Captain Messervy.

The schooner *Trader* was forced ashore at Willunga on 6 September and sold as a wreck to Captain Wells who attempted to salvage her. When he was unsuccessful the ship eventually became a total loss. Built in 1854, the *Trader* was a wooden vessel of 151 tons on dimensions of 95.7ft x 24ft x 8.8ft, registered at Port Adelaide

The brigantine *Letty*, with a general cargo, ran ashore at Red Cliffs near Port Augusta on 11 November. Refloated, she was found to be too badly damaged to repair so was towed to Port Augusta and broken up. Originally a paddle steamer at Williamstown in Victoria, the *Letty* was converted to sail and registered at Port Adelaide. She was a wooden vessel of 158 tons, measuring 99.9 x 24.9 x 12.7 ft.

An unconfirmed report said that the 29 ton schooner *Thistle* was lost near Cape Jervis during 1866.

1867

The wreck of the barque *Zanoni* has attracted considerable attention in recent times due principally to interest in its composite construction of iron and wood, and also because it was intact when lost. In April 1983 retired fisherman Rex Tyrell took divers Ian O'Donnell and John McGovern to investigate what appeared to be a reef near Ardrossan. It was the *Zanoni,* still relatively intact.

Now protected under the Historic Shipwrecks Act it is visited regularly by divers and archaeologists carrying out surveys and excavations.

When the *Zanoni* arrived in Adelaide in February 1861 with a cargo of sugar from Mauritius she was immediately chartered to load wheat for England. After loading the bulk of her cargo at Port Wakefield she left on 11 February, but shortly after sailing a violent storm struck with little warning throwing the *Zanoni* on her beam ends;then rolling her over.

The Victor Harbour Rocket Apparatus shooting the rocket, 3 March 1894. (From the original photograph by A.J.Humberstone, Photographer, Victor Harbour. Loaned by Bill Hergstrom, Torquay).

As she sank the crew of thirteen escaped after righting a lifeboat that had drifted clear and were rescued that evening and taken on to Adelaide. Efforts to locate the wreck proved unsuccessful and its whereabouts were to remain a mystery for more than a century.

Built at Liverpool and registered there, the *Zanoni* was a composite three masted barque of 338 tons, measuring 139.2 x 23.4 x 14.6 feet.

The cutter *Agneta* with two aboard disappeared near Sultana Creek on 9 July.

1870

The cutter *Lady Ferguson,* sailed from Myponga for Aldinga with 192 bags of wheat. When entering her destination, she was found to be taking water, and the crew barely had time to take to the boats before she sank in about fifteen fathoms. She was built in 1868, of 17 tons.. Length 35.3ft; beam 11.6ft; depth 5.8ft.

On the morning of 4 April, the brig *Flying Cloud,* 235 tons, from Adelaide to Melbourne with a cargo of 5473 bags of sugar, went ashore off Cape Banks close to the remains of the *Admella.*

In a thick blanket of fog the crew believed they were at least ten miles out to sea when the vessel struck without warning on a reef and quickly broke in two. The crew, captain, his wife and child left in a boat and landed safely. Pieces from the ship drifted for many miles and some were reported as far east as Portland. The remains of the wreck brought a mere £5 at auction. The *Flying Cloud* was built in 1867 on dimensions of 105.9 x 26.5 x 13.6; Master Captain T. Urquhart.

The cutter *Walter & John* was reported lost off Point Bolingbroke on the evening of 21 February. Built at Port Adelaide in 1870 she was a cutter of 15 tons.

The cutter *Elizabeth* was lost off Whiting Point sometime in September.

1872

The master of the steamer *Black Diamond* was held responsible when his vessel stranded on Walrus Rock while steaming from Moonta Bay to Wallaroo on 25 May 1872.

A Court of Inquiry decided he did not give the necessary attention to the bearings of the Tipara light vessel, particularly when he also admitted that his compass was unreliable. His Certificate of Competency was suspended for six months.

The *Black Diamond* had first run ashore on Wilberta Reef between Wallaroo and Moonta, then after being refloated went aground a second time and was lost. She was a steamship of 159 tons, built at Pyrmont NSW in 1864 and measuring 122.1 x 19.1 x 6.1ft. She was owned by R.Towns of Sydney, her master being Captain Howes.

1873

The schooner *Kangaroo* went ashore on a reef north of Cape Elizabeth on 10 February during a voyage from Wynyard, Tasmania to Moonta Bay, and became a total loss.

When built at Kangaroo Island in 1855 she was a cutter of 36 tons but was considerably enlarged in 1863 to a two masted schooner of 58 tons on dimensions of 80.5 x 15.9 x 7.2ft.

The iron brig *Prince of Wales,* 238 tons, loaded with 1,500 bags of wheat blew ashore in MacDonnell Bay early on Friday 20 June during a south-westerly gale. In the high, sea she parted from the Government mooring and lodged on the reef between the wreck of the *Orwell* and Pinchgut Reef. The lifeboat was quickly alongside, but as she was not considered in any danger the crew remained on board.

Built at Aberdeen in 1845, the *Prince of Wales* was a vessel of 238 tons, registered in Sydney.

After a long career, the Government schooner *Flinders,* Captain McLachlan, master, was wrecked at Port MacDonnell.

She left Port Adelaide on 17 July to overhaul moorings and carry out routine work, but while anchored in Port MacDonnell Bay, sprang a leak and began to sink. Captain McLachlan ordered the moorings cut and the vessel beached. All the crew reached safety in her boat but the *Flinders* broke up rapidly.

Built 1863, 103 tons. Length 88.2ft, beam 20.7ft depth 8.2ft.

The cutter *Secret* was wrecked three miles north of Point Bollingbrooke on 20 July. She was a wooden cutter of 19 tons built at Hobart in 1851 and measuring 41.5 x 12.3 x 7ft.

CAPE JAFFA LIGHTHOUSE

Department of Transport photo.

The unique screw pile lighthouse at Cape Jaffa guided shipping along the treacherous south eastern coast for more than a century.

In 1974 the tower was presented to the National Trust at Kingston, and following re-erection and renovation it was officially handed over to them on 24 January, 1976.

Built in 1872 on the Margaret Brock Reef, the lighthouse was constructed on thirteen screw piles fastened into solid rock, awash at high tide.

Rising from the landing platform well above sea level were seven legs supporting the light which was accessible through a central iron column. The light was 100 feet above sea level. The lightkeepers' dwellings were also on the platform. The lighthouse was manned by two men with the relief based at Kingston in later years. In rough seas and high winds the structure moved alarmingly, a most disconcerting experience for casual visitors, although it was considered to be perfectly safe.

It witnessed tragedy and excitement. In 1917 the keepers rescued survivors from the tug *Nyora,* then in 1956, a report that the light was unmanned led to the discovery of the body of one of the keepers in the sea nearby. The other was never found and it was presumed both were drowned while fishing.

In the final hours of her voyage from London to Adelaide with thirty-two passengers and a general cargo, the *Iron King* struck Troubridge Shoal on the night of 11 December and became a total wreck.

After sighting the Troubridge Light the master, Captain White, decided to take soundings as his compasses appeared unreliable, but in doing so he ran the ship too close in with a heavy sea running and she went ashore. There was a slight panic among the passengers but when they calmed down Captain White landed them safely on Troubridge Island, then sent word of the wreck to Adelaide with the ketch *Edith Alice.*

Most of the ship's valuable cargo was recovered but the ship could not be saved. It was auctioned on 3 January and after being stripped of all fittings the hull was abandoned.

Built in 1867, the *Iron King* was a three masted iron ship of 871 tons measuring 196.7 x 31.5 x 19.f, registered at London.

1874

At about 4 am on 9 August, in hazy conditions, the barque *Fairfield,* in ballast from Port Adelaide to Wallaroo, struck rocks at Cape Cassini, Kangaroo Island, and soon became a total wreck. An inspection of the ship at daylight showed she was badly holed up forward and had lost her rudder. A boat was lowered, and when a line was fastened all the crew reached safety. After resting with local settlers for several days the crew returned to Adelaide in the ship's boat and a salvage crew, sent to the scene in the paddle tug *Eleanor,* were able to recover most of her gear and stores.

A Court of Inquiry found that the loss of the *Fairfield* was caused by fault and neglect of the master and his certificate was suspended for six months. Built at New York in 1846, the *Fairfield* was a wooden barque of 534 tons on dimensions of 138.5 x 30.5 x 17.9ft, valued at £5000 but insured for only £2000. She was owned by H.Simpson & Company of Adelaide, her master being J. Taylor.

During a heavy gale, a cargo of potatoes carried by the schooner *Adelaide* shifted, throwing her on her beam ends. The foremast was cut away to steady her but in falling it brought down the mainmast, and the helpless vessel drifted ashore on the Coorong. A seaman named Joseph Roberts swam ashore with a line but the mate who was assisting him was drowned. The remainder of the crew eventually reached safety.

She was built originally as a paddle steamer in 1849; altered to a two masted ketch 1861. 61 tons. Length 72ft, beam 15.8ft, depth 8.3ft.

Mystery surrounds the fate of the small schooner *Triumph* which left Port MacDonnell in October, headed eastwards, but was not seen again. It is supposed she was lost near the mouth of the Glenelg River, although another report says she was lost near the Murray. She was built in 1863, of 46 tons. Length 64.7ft, beam 15.3ft, depth 7.7ft.

The barque *Wave Queen,* 250 tons, left Port Adelaide for Rivoli Bay on August 19th and two days later, when only a short distance from her destination was forced east to Cape Bridgewater by a gale. Captain Heslop worked her back to Cape Northumberland but she was again driven to the east. She returned a second time and anchored in the bay on 2 September to take on bags of flour.

Bad weather delayed loading, but on the 6th, one of her cables parted and she eventually drove ashore. Despite the rough seas three hands reached the shore, but the master, officers and crew remained on board until the main deck was under water. During breaks in the weather, yards, masts, sails, and some cargo were removed.

Built in 1861. Length 118.ft, beam 24.ft, depth 14.7ft.

While Lying at Wallaroo on 11 May the colliers *Kadina* and *Wallaroo,* both employed by the Black Diamond Line of H.Simpson & Sons of Port Adelaide were destroyed by a gale.

The *Kadina* had been hauled clear of the wharf as a precaution against possible bad weather and plans had been prepared for her to proceed to Port Adelaide, unload about 340 tons of coal, then be placed on the slip.

The *Wallaroo* with 700 tons of coal was lying a short distance from her receiving the full force of the gale when suddenly without warning her chains parted and she drove across the bow of the *Kadina,* smashing her own bowsprit and jib-boom, then losing the top of her foremast before going hard aground.

The jib-boom of the *Kadina* was smashed and her cables were also cut. She too went ashore close by the *Wallaroo* about 100 yards off the beach.

While anchored in Antechamber Bay, Kangaroo Island on 7 June, the schooner *Albert* broke from her moorings and drifted ashore where she became a total wreck. Build in 1863, of 19 tons. Length 45.8ft; beam 12.4ft; depth 5ft.

The cutter *Nimrod* foundered near the Port Adelaide lighthouse on the night of 26 July, taking with her the owner/master William Nelson whose body was never found. The submerged wreck was a danger to other vessels until it finally broke up in January of the following year. The *Nimrod,* 12 tons was built at Port Adelaide in 1866.

The ketch *Rose* left Port Adelaide for Yankalilla on 10 December but capsized when off Normanville. No lives were lost. The steamer *Glenelg* later located the vessel partly submerged but little was salvaged. Built in 1875, of 43 tons. Length 64ft; beam 18ft; depth 6ft.

1876

An explosion in a tank of gunpowder on the deck of the *Malvina Maud* destroyed her on 20 February, a short time after a fire had broken out on board while she was anchored at Port Pirie. The captain and crew jumped overboard a short time before the schooner blew up, but the captain was not seen again. Built at Battery Point on the Tamar River in 1815, the *Malvina Maud* was a vessel of 51 tons, registered at Launceston.

WRECKERS AND SMUGGLERS

Wreckers and smugglers were not a major problem for Customs Officers in South Australia nevertheless law breakers occasionally came under notice.

Unsubstantiated rumours circulated after the loss of two vessels near Port MacDonnell late in 1874. First, the schooner *The Triumph* disappeared between Port MacDonnell and Port Adelaide late in August and when her remains were found east of the Glenelg River in mid October the press insinuated that local residents had plundered everything of value found on shore before reporting the discovery. Nothing was ever proved.

At about the same time, while the barque *Wave Queen* was loading at Rivoli Bay she was forced ashore by bad weather on 6 September and lost.

There were few reports of illegal salvagers then, but two years later when controversy was raging concerning the possible involvement of Rivoli Bay residents in the plundering of the *Geltwood,* mention was made of their activities at the *Wave Queen.*

The barque *Glenrosa* was bound from Gravesend to Brisbane with a general cargo when she stranded on a shoal near Cape Banks on 18 January. After she was sold by auction, *S.S.Grace Darling* was sent from Adelaide to salvage as much cargo as possible and a number of local men were employed bringing the goods ashore. When they showed an interest in salvaging a little on their own account the new owner of the wreck allowed them to carry ashore as much clothing as they could wear. Among the items they collected were large cases of moleskin trousers, very popular at that time as working men's trousers. One man struggled into six pairs and was so restricted in the stiff board like pants that he fell overboard. Eventually, half drowned, he was hauled aboard the shore boat so stiff in his wet clothing that he had to lie flat out in the bottom of the boat. However, he managed to save the pants.

There is no record of the attitude of the purchasers of the cargo to the owner of the wreck giving away their goods; perhaps their comments were unprintable.

See also the wreck of the *Geltwood,* 1876.

On 31 March, the brigantine *Galatea,* Captain Garson, master, went ashore at Port MacDonnell during a gale and became a total loss. Loaded with general cargo, she broke away from her moorings during the night and drove on to the beach east of the jetty. The crew launched a boat and reached the shore, but within a few hour the *Galatea* had been completely destroyed, although some of her cargo was salvaged.

Built at Bremen in 1860, of 178 tons. Length 92.7ft; beam 21.5ft; depth 11.9ft.

GELTWOOD

The ill fated barque *Geltwood*. (Millicent Museum).

The barque *Geltwood* left Liverpool, England on 23 March with twenty-seven passengers, also 1000 tons of general cargo for Sydney and Melbourne, and had been 75 days at sea when apparently struck by a tremendous storm when off the south eastern coast of South Australia, disabled, then driven ashore.

A few settlers apparently saw distress rockets far out to sea but as nothing could be done to help dismissed the incident and then forgot to report it to local authorities.

Some time later a boundary rider named Sparks searching for cattle along the coastline about five miles from Cunanda Station, fourteen miles from Millicent, stumbled across wreckage and human remains in the sand.

The partially decomposed body of a man of about 40 years of age carried a tattoo on the right arm consisting of the words "R.W.S.Dundee 1852", enclosed in a wreath with the British Arms and the Union Jack.

Wreckage scattered over several hundred metres included two smashed life boats, one intact whale boat, barrels of ale, lifebuoys, cases of crockery, tobacco and piles of splintered timber. The hull could be seen rising up and down in a cleft in the reef about 1000 metres from the shore.

Searching for survivors from the wrecked barque *Geltwood*, 1876.
(Author's Collection).

Delicate porcelain figures recoverd from the remains of the *Geltwood*. Other
artefacts brought up from the wreck include portholes, bottles of stout, vases,
plates, an anchor and numerous other items.   (Author's Collection).

Portion of the bowsprit and a few spars appeared to be still attached to it, but searchers could not approach due to the ceaseless surge.

Inland from the beach they found tracks of bullock drays in the scrub, then stumbled across a cache of sixty boxes of tobacco and a seaman's chest bearing the name "E.S.Burnett".

Discreet inquiries revealed that about a dozen settlers had apparently been involved plundering the wreck, caring little for the scene of death and terrible destruction as they loaded their wagons with goods and set out for their homes. Fred Barrien appeared to be the ring leader. Police searched his house and found goods valued at more than £200,

Reward notice posted after extensive looting of the *Geltwood* wreck.

including calico, cloth, prints, stockings, spoons and tobacco. A second plant was found buried in his father's cow shed. A brother surrendered articles of brushware and a sailor's chest filled with sundries.

Grave of one of the few bodies recovered from the wreck of the *Geltwood,* in the Millicent cemetery. (Millicent Museum).

Barrien was fined £10 in default two months imprisonment, while Louis Spehr, tanner of Millicent also appeared charged with stealing cargo. His tan pits at Millicent held a plant of tobacco, but as they had flooded, the tobacco was useless. Locals however thought the remains would make an excellent sheep dip.

The *Geltwood,* an iron barque of 1056 tons, was launched at Harrington, England in January 1876 on dimensions of 215.7 x 33.9 x 21.1ft., and intended for the Australia-San Francisco trade. Built by Messrs Williamson she was owned by Captain Sprott, the master being Captain Harrington who also had an interest in her. Her cargo valued at £18,000 was insured for £10,000. She was on her maiden voyage when lost.

An anchor from the *Geltwood* provides the focal point for a display featuring the wreck in the Millicent Museum.

A sketch from the "Australian News" depicting the loss of the schooner *Agnes* near Cape Jaffa on the night of 13 March, 1865.
(Author's Collection).

The barque *Agnes,* loaded with coal from Newcastle to Adelaide went ashore near Cape Banks on 18 July. The ship was doomed from the instant she struck and when a boat containing nine members of the crew swamped immediately it was lowered they only regained the temporary safety of the barque after a long, hard battle.

Eventually four of them reached the shore and set out for the Cape Northumberland lighthouse where they were given shelter while help was summoned. *S.S. City of Hobart* towed the Port MacDonnell lifeboat to the wreck which was breaking up in the heavy sea. William Holland, the mate, swam across from the barque to the lifeboat with a line attached to a lifebuoy and this allowed four men still on board to cross to safety shortly before the vessel crumpled fore and aft. The master, H. Smidt was held responsible for the loss and his certificate was suspended for twelve months.

She was a wooden barque of 330 tons, built at Baltimore USA in 1860 on dimensions of 126.3 x 27.6 x 12.1ft, and owned by P. Manuel.

The schooner *Countess,* 83 tons was wrecked at Port MacDonnell on 16 August, but no lives were lost. She was at anchor in the bay when her moorings parted in a heavy gale and she was driven on to the beach. Her remains lay on the beach for many years before removal as a hazard at night to fishermen. Built in 1875, of dimensions 73 x 19 x 7.6ft.

During a gale at Port MacDonnell on 28 September, the barque *St. Marc* parted from the Government moorings and despite prompt efforts to work her out to sea, drifted ashore near Cress Creek where heavy seas made a clean breach over her, breaking off the mainmast and driving the crew to the poop. A lifeboat went off and succeeded in rescuing the crew of fourteen shortly before the barque broke in two. The efforts of the lifeboat crew were recognised by the French Government who later presented them with medals and certificates of appreciation.

The *St.Marc* was a French vessel of 269 tons register with Captain Joycin as master.

On the 23 October a farmer living south of Millicent heard gun shots from the direction of Carpenter's Rocks. Four days later a body was found washed up on the beach and in early November the heel of the lower mast of a small vessel of about 40 tons drifted ashore near the Cape Northumberland lighthouse.

The sailing barge *Sarah* was crossing from Point Lowly to Port Pirie with a cargo of bluestone on 21 December when she sprang a leak. After being run ashore the crew left to obtain help.

The schooner *Cygnet* was lost near Rivoli Bay. Built 1875, of 74 tons. Length 19ft; beam 20ft; depth 7.8ft.

1877

While on a voyage to Wool Bay, the schooner *Rambler,* 24 tons, damaged her rigging and would not answer the helm. An anchor was let go but it dragged and she went ashore on the 19 January.

Sailing from Albany to Port Adelaide with thirty-nine passengers and crew, also a mixed cargo, the brigantine *Emily Smith* was driven off course by rough weather and forced ashore on the rugged west coast of Kangaroo Island at about 4.30 a.m. on the morning of 15 May. The brigantine broke up rapidly and only five survived to reach the shore, where they split up to seek help. Eventually, three reached the Cape Borda lighthouse and while a search was mounted for the other two, word of the wreck was telegraphed to Adelaide and the Government steamer *Governor Musgrave* was sent. Only a few bodies were found in the surf near the wreck, while the two who had survived to reach the beach were not seen alive again. Built 1849, of 129 tons. Length 87.5ft; beam 19.5ft; depth 12ft.

The schooner *Freebridge,* on her regular run to ports on the west coast parted her anchors while sheltering in Waterloo Bay and went ashore on 12 June. Passengers and crew reached safety. Built in 1850 she was a wooden schooner of 92 tons, registered at Port Adelaide.

Five lives were lost when the brig *Edith Haviland,* 264 tons, was wrecked on Carpenter's Reef on 18 June. The vessel was sailing between Adelaide and Sydney with a cargo of flour when she went ashore in hazy weather. The captain, J. Roddy and six of his crew floated ashore on portion of the deck as the vessel broke up, but Mrs. Roddy and her three children drowned. The fifth casualty occurred when a member of the crew was carried out by the undertow after reaching the beach in a lifebelt. Built in 1865. Length 114.4ft; beam 25.5ft; depth 14.4ft.

EARLY HAZARDS IN BACKSTAIRS PASSAGE

The rapid, and sometimes irregular tidal stream which often exceeds four knots presented problems for sail and early low powered steamers using Backstairs Passage, the narrow strait separating the eastern end of Kangaroo Island and the Fleurieu Peninsula on the South Australian mainland.

In the south eastern approaches a group of rugged islets and rocks known as The Pages, almost in the centre of the channel were a potential hazard, and to the north west, Yatala Shoal was also a danger. Wrecks and strandings were not the only hazards around the shores of Backstairs Passage.

At about midnight on 20 November, 1854, as the new 229 ton steamer *Champion,* on her delivery voyage to the Henty Brothers at Portland was entering Backstairs Passage in the face of a heavy gale, she collided with *P.S.Melbourne,* 115 tons, bound from Port Elliot to Adelaide. Although the *Champion* received only minor damage the *Melbourne* was so badly disabled that she was taken in tow by the *Champion* which returned her to Adelaide before continuing her voyage. Three years later the *Champion* was lost in a collision with *S.S.Lady Bird* off Cape Otway, Victoria.

The following year the steamers *Burra Burra,* 122 tons, and the *White Swan,* 322 tons collided off Cape Jervis on the night of 3 November. The *Burra Burra* lost her bowsprit and foretopmast, also damaging her cutwater, while the *White Swan* was badly damaged on the port bow. Both vessels were soon repaired and returned to service.

On the night of 19 January, 1857, the *White Swan* was in another collision in Backstairs Passage, again off Cape Jervis. This time she badly damaged the 82 ton schooner *Agnes* which was forced to return to Adelaide for repairs.

In the same year, as the schooner *Swallow,* from Swan River, was leaving Encounter Bay after sheltering from a gale during a voyage to Adelaide, she collided with the schooner *Valentine Helicar* which was lying at anchor. The *Swallow* lost her starboard bulwarks and stanchions while the *Valentine Helicar* lost portion of her figurehead, topsail yard and some rigging.

The last major collision in and around Backstairs Passage appears to have occurred in 1874 when the 414 ton steamer *Penola* and the 56 ton yacht *Hygeia* collided off Cape Jervis on the night of 21 December, but suffered only minor damage.

The schooner *Fanny Wright,* on her way to Eucla with telegraph poles, called at Waterloo Bay on 7 August to pick up cargo salvaged from the *Freebridge,* when she accidentally struck one of the wrecked vessel's anchors and commenced to leak. She was run ashore but was found to be too badly damaged to repair. Built at Brisbane Water in 1873 she was a vessel of 103 tons, registered at Port Adelaide.

The steam launch *Tipara* foundered near Wardang Island on 2 September while under tow.

The barge *Lady Of The Lake,* 18 tons, dragged ashore at Port Victor during a gale on 3 October and was lost.

The cutter *Wildflower* capsized off Port Adelaide on 11 November drowning her crew of two.

1878

The schooner *Young St.George,* 15 tons, was wrecked at the Althorpe Islands on 3 January.

Was the brigantine *Salve* beached at Port Pirie and lost on 25 October?

The schooner *Louise,* 29 tons, broke her moorings at Port Rickaby during November and was lost.

The cutter *James and Margaret* was destroyed by fire at Telowie Beach on 6 December.

1879

The barque *Ismyr* left Port Pirie on 16 February bound for England with wheat. Apparently she grounded on a reef off Reef Head on the 24th but managed to free herself. When entering Port Pirie to load in January she had also run aground but was refloated undamaged.
After 241 days out the *Ismyr* was posted missing at Lloyds and shipping authorities believed the two strandings must have caused major damage which probably caused her to founder in heavy weather.
The *Ismyr* was an iron barque of 610 tons built at Liverpool in 1868 on dimensions of 171.8 x 27.9 x 17.5 ft.

The barge *Four Brothers* sprang a leak and foundered at Port Wakefield on 26 March. She was refloated and towed around to Adelaide, but was apparently too badly damaged to be returned to service. She was a wooden vessel of 43 tons, built in 1851 and measuring 54 x 18 x 5.7ft.

Fire destroyed the hulk *Kadina* at Port Adelaide in the early hours of 20 April. The flames were first noticed at about 2a.m. and the fire gradually gained control of the interior. First, the mainmast went overboard, then the planking was burnt away from the timbers, leaving only her framework. By daylight, when the poop ignited the whole ship was afire, with only the foremast still standing, then only the chain plates were left to show the position of each mast. During the morning a tug towed the smouldering hulk as high on the shore as possible.
The *Kadina* was a barque of 661 tons, built in 1853 on dimensions of 149 x 31 x 21.7ft. She had been wrecked at Wallaroo four years earlier,then refloated and hulked. (See entry under 1875.)

The cutter *Maria* disappeared near Port Adelaide on 16 June. Some wreckage was recovered on the beach at Semaphore, but the mystery was never solved. She was apparently unregistered.

1860

The barque *Southern Cross*, lost near Cape Douglas in 1880.
(Author's Collection).

The barque **Southern Cross**, 435 tons, a well-known trader around
the Australian coast was wrecked near Cape Douglas on 7 January,
after land was mistaken for a cloud and the vessel struck an outlying
reef before the mistake was discovered. Fortunately the sea was
moderate and the crew left safely in the boats although the vessel
became a total wreck. Her remains are still visible on the beach.

A Court of Inquiry blamed currents for the wreck but believed a
better lookout should have been kept. Built in 1851, of 435 tons gross,
345 tons net. Length 144ft; beam 26ft; depth 14ft.

After leaving Port Pirie on 19 January bound for the United
Kingdom, the **Lady Kinnaird** went ashore on Cape Burr in Spencer's
Gulf after being buffeted by a southerly gale. The crew were rescued
after some anxious moments but there was no hope of saving the ship.
She lay about half a mile off shore with her stern immersed at high
water and the whole of her cargo of 35,508 bushels of wheat ruined.
The master hurried to Adelaide to report the wreck, leaving the crew
camped on the beach about fifteen miles from Warratta Vale, living on
provisions washed ashore.

A Marine Board Inquiry was of the opinion that the master
negligently navigated his ship on the night she was lost but no action
was taken against him. Underwater survey teams have examined this

NARROW ESCAPES

The stranded steamer *Sorata* at Cape Jervis, September 1880.
(State Library of South Australia, 1976).

In the years 1880-81, two famous steamers operating in the England - Australia trade narrowly escaped disaster on the South Australian coast near Adelaide.

The *Sorata* made her first appearance in Australian waters in April 1879 when the Orient Line introduced fortnightly sailings to Australia, still using chartered steamers owned by the Pacific Steam Navigation Company. On 3 September 1880 she arrived at Adelaide from London, via Cape Town, in 37 days, then left for Melbourne with 368 passengers and a cargo which included exhibits for the International Exhibition, soon to open at the Exhibition Building in Melbourne.

The sea was smooth, and the weather fine with a light haze as she passed through Backstairs Passage where a strong ebb tide forced her unexpectedly on to the Yatala Shoal, about 3 kilometres south of Cape Jervis. Distress signals were raised and the boats lowered without delay. When *S.S.Woonona* hove in sight at about 10 p.m., all female passengers and some males were transferred across. Several boat loads were also sent to the Cape Jervis lighthouse while the remainder spent the night on deck.

Next day, all passengers returned on board while several vessels tried vainly to free the vessel, and when the weather began to deteriorate the passengers left her, while some cargo was unloaded and sent to Adelaide for transhipment.

Water began to rise in several compartments and a diver went down to examine the outside of the hull about midships forward on the port side. He found little apparent damage, but as the *Sorata*

---

continued to take water into the hold, and the swell increased, hopes of saving her faded. The owners were determined that every effort would be made to save the *Sorata*. Diver Ericson who had successfully completed salvage on the barque *Geltwood* was hastily summoned, while the Orient Line sent out a salvage expert named Armit, and his gear, on board *S.S.Cotopaxi*.

Despite the heavy seas pounding the ship *Ericson* was able to seal the holes in her hull, and when Armit arrived, his powerful steam pumps soon had her afloat once again. The paddle tug *Albatross* towed her to Adelaide for temporary repairs, then she proceeded to Melbourne and entered the Alfred Graving Dock on 9 December, the largest vessel to enter it up to that time.

On 9 January of the following year the Orient steamer *Chimborazo*, inward bound to Port Adelaide from London ran on to Marion Reef near Troubridge Shoal after confusing navigation lights in foggy conditions. Authorities still smarting over the near loss of the *Sorata* only a short distance away were relieved when she was refloated next day after some cargo had been removed. When the *Chimborazo* docked in Sydney there was no evidence of damage.

---

wreck closely in recent years; in March 1979 her main anchor was recovered and prepared for display.

The *Lady Kinnaird* was an iron barque of 680 tons burthen, built at Dundee in 1877, measuring 190 x 30.4 x 17.8ft. Her master was Captain A. Laws.

The brig *Byron*, 174 tons, dismasted in a squall off Kangaroo Island on 22 May while on a voyage from Fremantle to Adelaide was towed to Adelaide for conversion to a hulk.

In August the ketch *Premaydena* left Port MacDonnell for Adelaide but was not seen again, despite an intensive search. Built in 1870, of 50 tons. Length 69.2ft; beam 18.2ft; depth 5.5ft.

The 13 ton cutter *Edith,* with no one aboard, blew ashore at Wallaroo on the night of 21 October during a south westerly gale.

1881

A severe squall off the Althorpe Islands on 8 May capsized the schooner *Experiment* with the loss of the captain and a seaman. The mate and cook managed to launch a boat and reached Kangaroo Island. Built in 1814 the *Experiment* was a wooden vessel of 55 tons, registered at Port Adelaide.

One life was lost when the steamer *Euro* struck rocks near Beachport on 24 August. The *Euro* was steaming close in to shore when she was so badly holed on a submerged reef that her master Captain Dowell, decided the only hope was to beach her. Full steam was maintained for as long as possible, then two boats were cast off shortly before she sank, leaving only her masts and funnel above water.

Those left on the wreck clung to the rigging and funnel until rescued. One boat overturned in the surf but no lives were lost despite the heavy seas. It was not until a check of passengers and crew was taken some time later that a lady passenger was missed, and it was assumed she had drowned when the vessel sank.

Once news of the wreck reached Beachport help was quickly sent although a few of the survivors struggled overland to the settlement. A Marine Court of Inquiry later cleared Captain Dowell of any blame for the wreck.

Built 1814, 461 tons gross. Length 165.4ft; beam 23.2ft; depth 10.5ft.

The ketch *Ark* was abandoned in Spencer Gulf on 11 November while on a voyage from Port Germein to Port Adelaide with bagged wheat. The crew reached Port Lincoln safely in a small boat. The *Ark*, 45 tons, built in 1813 was registered at Port Adelaide.

1882

The steam launch *Helen* was wrecked at Carpenter Rocks on the night of 9 February, without loss of life.

The cutter *Dart* was lost at Myponga on 28 March, once again without loss of life.

A strong northerly gale blew the cutter *Parara* ashore near Point Lowly in Spencer Gulf on 10 July while she was preparing to unload building materials for the lighthouse. Built in 1814 she was a vessel of 35 tons.

The brig *Miss Kilmansegg* was so badly damaged when driven ashore by a gale near Semaphore on 29 September she was not repaired after being refloated. Built at Dumbarton in 1863, she was a wooden vessel of 229 tons, registered at Port Adelaide.

While on a voyage from Port Victoria to Moonta the ketch *Young Lion* was wrecked on the Cape Elizabeth Reef on 18 October. There was no loss of life. Built in 1874, the *Young Lion* was a vessel of 31 tons.

The hull of a vessel of about 60 tons was sighted by *S.S. Glenelg* about nine miles north west of Cape Jaffa. It was never identified.

The Chinese influence on Robe and the goldfields is indicated on this plaque on the Robe foreshore which reads: "During the years 1856 to 1858, 16500 Chinese landed near this spot and walked 200 miles to Ballarat and Bendigo in search of gold." (P.Stone photo).

1883

Following a collision with the schooner *Grace Darling* off Four Hummocks Island in the early hours of 8 February, the schooner *Amelia* sank. Her crew of eight quickly crossed to the *Grace Darling* and were later landed safely After some cargo was salvaged the wreck was forced into deep water and lost. Built in 1858 the *Amelia* was a vessel of 25 tons.

The wooden steamer ***Little Orient*** blew up at Adelaide on 20 November while steam was being raised. She was a vessel of 23 tons, built in Sydney in 1879, measuring 54.8 x 12 5.3ft.

SMALL CRAFT MISHAPS

This illustration of the capsizing of the mail boat at Port Adelaide in 1865 shows one of the hazards sometimes faced by small craft along the South Australian coastline.

The loss of a cutter from *H.M.S. Investigator* on 21 February, 1802, while Flinders was exploring the coastline in the vicinity of present day Port Lincoln was one of the earliest disasters to small craft. A water party, comprising two officers and a crew of six left the ship to land on the mainland and was not seen again. A boat sent to search for them failed to find any trace.

The disappearance of two men off the south west coast of Kangaroo Island in 1885 was also associated with a small boat mishap. Four local men commenced sealing near Cape du Couedic, and their system was to have two of their number camped on one of the rugged and almost inaccessible Casuarina Islets, known as The Brothers, and really little more than barren rocks, while the other two kept their boat nearby in a small inlet on the main island.

Each day, the two men with the boat delivered wood and water to the men on the islets and returned with sealskins. One day after leaving their companions the men in the boat rowed east along the rugged coastline towards the Remarkable Rocks and were never seen again, although their damaged boat was later discovered in Hanson Bay, several kilometres to the east.

1884

The *Hero* was lost at Glenelg on 20 January.

The cutter *Treasure Trove* was lost at Kingston on 21 May.

The *Alternative,* 15 tons, went on to rocks in Memory Cove on 24 September and became a total loss.

Loaded with 1,200 tons of coal for Wallaroo, the barque *Fanny M* ran into adverse winds when approaching Backstairs Passage between Kangaroo Island and the mainland and was eventually forced ashore a few miles north east from Kingscote on 15 May. Coal was jettisoned in an attempt to refloat her but she remained fast until destroyed by a fire in mysterious circumstances two days later.
The *Fanny M,* a composite vessel of 678 tons, measuring 159.3 x 32.2 x 18.2ft, was built at Carleton, New Brunswick, USA in 1877. Her master was Captain Stockton.

In ballast from Melbourne to Port Pirie, the barque *Mars* was driven ashore on Kangaroo Island in the early hours of 15 June. When she struck, three of the crew were washed overboard and lost, but eventually a sailor swam ashore and fastened a line which helped eight of the crew to land. Several days later three of them reached the lighthouse on Cape Borda and notified the head keeper of the wreck.
Helped by the keepers the survivors reached the lighthouse on 24 June and were later taken on to Adelaide aboard the steamer *Lady Diana.* The *Mars* was a wooden vessel of 487 tons, built in 1877. She measured 150 x 29.9 x 16.8ft. Her master, Robert Pringle was lost in the wreck.

The unregistered ketch *Daring* was wrecked in the Hog Bay Basin on 10 August when she struck an anchor left by the vessel *H.P.Bates* in the fairway. G.Phillips, the captain, and one man, saved equipment and goods before she sank. The ketch and her cargo were uninsured.

Pilot McCarthy was cruising down Spencers Gulf in the cutter *Mary Ann* early in December when the man steering called that water was running into her hold. All hands manned the pump but they were forced into the dinghy when about fifteen miles south-west of Mount Young. After two days battling adverse conditions they were rescued off Black Point and taken to Port Augusta. The *Mary Ann* was registered at Port Augusta and insured for £200.

1886

The cutter *Annie Watt* was destroyed by fire at Port Germein on 4 April.

The yacht *Minnie* was lost at Glenelg on 22 April.

The fishing boat *Pioneer* was sheltering from a gale in Marion Bay on the Yorke Peninsula when forced ashore and lost on 24 July.

The two masted schooner *Ewbank,* 17 tons was lost on the south coast of Kangaroo Island.

1887

The barque *Kebroyd* sprang a leak on 13 February while on her way to Western Australia and was run ashore in Anxious Bay. She was refloated, and towed to Port Adelaide, where she was converted into a hulk. Built in 1866 the *Kebroyd* was a wooden vessel of 353 tons, registered at Port Adelaide.

The fishing boat *Harriet* disappeared at sea during May.

The cutters *Red Rover* and *Athens* disappeared near Port Lincoln late in September.

The Norwegian barque *Guldax,* laden with timber, 108 days out from Sweden with timber, dragged her anchors in a gale and went ashore near Normanville on 2 September. She struck with tremendous force bringing down all her masts and rigging, except the mizzen. Two boats were launched and one reached safety, but the second turned back when it seemed it would be overwhelmed by the huge seas. Heavy seas battered the wreck and she appeared in imminent danger of breaking up. The tug *Yatala* arrived next day and eventually all the crew were taken off.

On 14 September rough weather forced the *Guldax* closer in shore where she broke up after much of her cargo had been salvaged. At auction the remains brought £36.

The *Guldax* was a vessel of 556 tons measuring approx. 149 x 21.1 x 18.3ft. She was built in Norway in 1878.

1888

While Captain Maas, his wife, children and the crew were asleep on board the wheat laden barque *Saturn* at Port Pirie on the morning of 7 January, a fire broke out in the lazarette and soon enveloped the entire ship.

The alarm was given by the captain's daughter who was wakened by the smoke, and the crew quickly lowered the boats. All three were damaged and sunk by the crew who panicked and rushed into them with their luggage.

Fortunately, boats from the barques *Copesfield* and *Aretas* took all to safety. Meanwhile, the stricken vessel was towed to Cockle's Spit and left to burn to the water's edge.

The *Saturn* was a vessel of 484 tons register built at Stralsund, Prussia in 1877. She had called at Adelaide before proceeding to Port Pirie where she loaded more wheat to make a total of 5483 bags before going out to the anchorage to await orders. The cargo was insured for £800 but the vessel was only partly covered.

The Inquiry into the fire recorded, "The fire broke out in the lazarette but there is no evidence to show how it originated".

The ketch *Young E.B.*, 23 tons, was wrecked near Marino Rocks on 30 June.

STAR OF GREECE

Artist's impression of the total loss of the ship *Star of Greece* near Port Willunga, 13 July 1888.

Eleven seamen lost their lives when the three-masted iron ship, *Star of Greece*, with a crew of twenty-eight, was wrecked off Port Willunga on Friday, July 13th. Under the command of Captain H. Harrower, she arrived at Port Adelaide after an eighty-six-day voyage out from England. Cargo unloaded included two cannon ordered for Glenelg because of the fears of a Russian invasion which were currently sweeping the colonies.

She then loaded 16,002 bags of wheat for London and prepared for the long voyage home. She set sail in fine, but threatening weather, and late in the evening ran into a north-westerly gale which drove her twenty miles off course and ashore about 200 yards off the beach at Port Willunga. Raging seas and driving winds battered the doomed vessel forcing many of the crew into the mizzen rigging. Before dawn the foremast went over the side and the ship commenced to break up.

Attempts to lower a lifeboat failed, but during the morning most of the officers and crew battled their way to the bows where they found a little protection from the raging seas. About mid-morning, the ship broke in two amidships, and the after section, with eight men clinging in the rigging, disappeared. Men began leaping into the sea. Some reached the shore but three of these died from exhaustion after landing. Others disappeared in the raging seas.

96

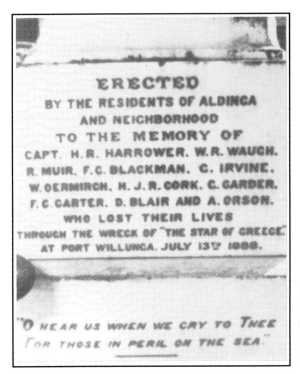

Marble obelisk at
Aldinga, built to
remember those lost
in the wreck of the
Star of Greece.
(Author's
Collection).

Vessels sent from Port Adelaide were powerless while bad roads, poor telegraphic communications and difficulty in procuring a good vehicle and horses delayed the arrival of the rocket gear until it was too late. For days the search for bodies was carried out along the beach which was littered with wreckage, provisions and cargo. Later, the press strongly criticised the rescue operations, but the widespread indignation and shame did stimulate support for a fund opened to assist those saved and the dependants of the victims.

A preliminary inquiry held by the Marine Board found that the vessel was mishandled after leaving port and that the lead should have been used more when the ship was drifting. As the master had lost his life, and no blame was attached to the mate, the case was not referred to a Court of Inquiry. There was also no proof of a report that there was drunkenness on board.

Constable Tuohy of Willunga, who played a prominent part in rescue operations, received the Royal Humane Society's silver medal and a gold medal presented by the South Australian Government.

Today, most signs of the wreck have disappeared, and its exact location is known to a few divers. However, there are many interesting relics and mementoes from the ship in the district and at Adelaide.

The *Star of Greece* was built in 1868, of 1257 tons gross, 1193 tons net. Length 227ft; beam 35ft; depth 22.2ft.

Little remains of the *Star of Greece* underwater.
(Photo:P.Stone, Seadive).

1889

S.S.Cowry was lost near Normanville on 5 June when forced ashore by a gale. She had arrived from Adelaide the previous day and immediately commenced to discharge cargo. During the night the wind freshened and next day when heavy seas almost swamped her she was abandoned. The *Cowry* was a wooden vessel of 27 tons, built in 1879.

1890

The barque *Glenrosa* was bound from England to Brisbane with a general cargo when she ran ashore in a heavy fog a few miles east of Cape Banks on 18 January. While the weather remained calm she was in little danger, but all efforts to refloat her failed, and eventually heavy seas battered her to pieces although most of her cargo was salvaged after the hull was auctioned for £180 and the cargo £220. Captain E. Kerr was found guilty of careless navigation and lost his certificate for 18 months.

Built in 1875 on dimensions of 203.7 x 32.3 x 20ft, she was a barque of 869 tons.

On 14 June, *S.S.You Yangs,* well known in the Australian coastal trade, was lost on Kangaroo Island. She left Port Pirie for Sydney with a cargo of railway iron and flour but when east of Kangaroo Island some of her iron which was stowed on deck shifted, causing a dangerous list. Captain Veitch decided to return to Adelaide and was

The barque *Glenrosa* ashore near Cape Banks in January 1890. Efforts to refloat her failed and after most of her cargo had been salvaged she went to pieces. (Les Hill).

making reasonable progress when the steamer appeared to strike a rock on the south eastern side of the island and commenced taking water. The three lifeboats lowered were separated in the rising seas but all the crew were eventually located after a land and sea search. Some cargo was salvaged but the *You Yangs* broke up quickly.

A preliminary inquiry held at Adelaide decided that the shifting of the iron cargo had affected the ship's compasses and made the captain uncertain of his position. He had made an error in judgment in not taking shelter under the lee of the island until daybreak. However, no further action was taken.

The *You Yangs* was one of the early vessels on the Australian coast. She was built at London in 1856 and named *Kief,* then purchased in 1864 by William Howard Smith & Company for trade between Melbourne, Sydney and Tasmanian ports. She measured 690 tons on dimensions of 185.2 x 21.9 x 15ft.

The ketch *Ruby* disappeared between Salt Creek and Adelaide in July. Built in 1871, of 21 tons. Length 53ft; beam 16.1ft; depth 5ft.

1892

The ketch *Enterprise,* from Port Augusta to Port Adelaide with wheat foundered on 6 March after springing a leak off the Althorpe Islands. The crew pumped furiously but the water gained so they abandoned her. The *Enterprise* was a wooden ketch of 61 tons, built in 1883.

The ketch *Lotus* was wrecked at Port MacDonnell on 23 June when a gale parted her anchors while she was loading potatoes for Port Pirie. The lifeboat succeeded in rescuing the crew. Built at Port Adelaide in 1814, the *Lotus* was a wooden vessel of 91 tons.

The fishing cutter *Welling* was lost near the Althorpe Islands in July.

S.S.You Yangs, lost on Kangaroo Island, 1890.
(Author's Collection).

1893

A mistake in bearings by the master ran *S.S.Tenterden* on to Breaksea Reef west of Port MacDonnell near Cape Northumberland early in the morning of 23 December. The vessel left Melbourne and intended calling at Port MacDonnell to load 1300 bales of wool before proceeding to Beachport to load a further 500.

She arrived off the port at midnight, and Captain McEacharn decided to lie outside until daylight. However when she moved at about 3 a.m. she steamed onto the reef after ignoring several warnings, and remained fast. Heavy seas began to break over the vessel later in the day forcing the officers and crew to abandon her.

The tug *Albatross* was sent from Melbourne but once it was seen that the task of refloating her was hopeless, cabin fittings and all moveable equipment was landed. The wreck was distinct landmark until partly dismantled, then the sea did the rest. For many years the boilers remained but now they too have disappeared. A Court of Inquiry suspended Captain McEacharn's certificate for three months.

Built in 1883, of 1339 tons gross, 867 tons net. Length 246.5ft; beam 33.5ft; depth 19.9ft.

1894

The fishing cutter *Golden Hope* was lost in Nepean Bay, Kangaroo Island during March.

S.S. Tenterden, wrecked at Port MacDonnell in 1893.
(Author's Collection).

For many years the boilers from the *Tenterden* remained as a landmark after she was dismantled, but now they too have disappeared.
(Author's Collection).

The barque *Aeolus,* wrecked near Port MacDonnell in 1894.
(Author's Collection).

The barque *Aeolus* left Capetown, South Africa for Sydney on 3 August to load wool for England. On 1 September, 29 days out, in calm clear conditions she was sailing a short distance offshore near Cape Banks when a partially submerged reef was noticed ahead. Being in clay ballast the *Aeolus* was difficult to handle and after she missed stays an attempt to wear her had almost succeeded when she struck an outcrop of Carpenter Rocks, known as Agnes Reef after the vessel wrecked there in 1876, and remained fast.

As she struck, the reef ripped away plates along her port side and within a few minutes there was three feet of water in the hold and it continued to rise steadily. After some anxious moments the boats were lowered and all members of the crew landed safely on the beach. The *Aeolus* continued to grind heavily on the rocks, and with a strong list to port was totally abandoned with sails set. Within a week she was going to pieces after being auctioned for £30/10/-, with her lifeboat bringing £16 and captain's gig, £13.

At an Inquiry the Marine Board of South Australia found the master guilty of negligence and poor navigation, then suspended his certificate for six months.

The *Aeolus* was an iron ship of 1610 tons, built by Barclay, Earle & Company of Glasgow, Scotland in 1886 and owned by Carmichael & Company of Greenock. She measured 259.1 x 38.2 x 23ft. C. Campbell was her master.

The fishing cutter *Polly* was lost near Cape Jervis on 3 November.

Sightseers at the wreck of the *Aeolus* (background), 1894.
(Author's Collection).

1895

During a heavy gale the small wooden steamer, **Kingston**, moored at Port Caroline, blew ashore after losing her cables and was almost buried under sand and seaweed. A later inspection showed her to be beyond repair. Built in 1818, of 12 tons net. Length 55.5ft; beam 13.2ft; depth 5.8ft.

The yacht **Banshee** was lost at Wallaroo on 16 December.

1897

The cutter **Edith** struck rocks off the Sir Joseph Banks Group while fishing on 3 August and became a total wreck.

1898

From Port Augusta to the British Isles with 1165 tons of concentrates, the barque **Candida** ran ashore on Wardang Island on 20 February. Although eventually refloated on 10 April she was found to be too badly damaged to repair so was sold at auction for £300 and converted to a coal hulk. The **Candida** was originally an iron vessel of 1279 tons, built at Whitehaven, England in 1875 on dimensions of 226 x 36.1 x 22.1ft.

After leaving Port Adelaide for Lyttleton with a cargo of salt, the barque *Excelsior* called at Edithburgh only to run ashore off Salt Creek on 9 May. She was refloated and taken back to Port Adelaide where the estimated cost of repairs was so high she was converted into a hulk. Built in 1861 the *Excelsior* was a wooden vessel of 399 tons on dimensions of 128.5 x 27.1 x 16.3ft.

The 25 ton schooner *Ariel* was lying off Wedge Island on 14 May waiting to load guano when she dragged her anchors and went ashore, becoming a total wreck.

The cutter *Stranger,* 17 tons was also lost at Wedge Island about a month later when she broke her moorings near the wreck of the *Ariel* and went ashore. The crew of four swam to safety, and later, when crossing to the mainland in the cutter's dinghy they were picked up by the ketch *Eliza.*

1899

The yacht *Alice* was wrecked at Brighton Beach on 20 January.

The beautiful *Loch Sloy*, wrecked on Kangaroo Island with heavy loss of life, 1889. (Kendall Collection).

The barque *Loch Sloy,* carrying 34 passengers and crew, on a passage from Glasgow to Melbourne via Adelaide, ran ashore on the south west coast of Kangaroo Island on the morning of 24 April, after missing the Cape Borda light on the western end of the island.

The almost sheer cliffs on Kangaroo Island, near where the few survivors from the *Loch Sloy* came ashore.
(Kingscote Museum).

Those on board took refuge in the rigging as giant seas swept the decks, but as the masts collapsed most were hurled to their death. Only four reached the shore alive, battered by the cruel rocks and suffering from immersion. They then had great difficulty climbing the steep cliffs but managed to improvise a rope from blankets cut into strips, and eventually reached the top.

Seaman McMillan set out to search for assistance, but when he failed to return after three days the others decided to make for Cape Borda which they knew lay somewhere to the north. Shortly after setting out one of their party became too weak to continue and was left with a small supply of food.

On the night of 8 May, fifteen days after the wreck they saw the reflection of the Cape Borda light although they still had some distance to travel.

Meanwhile, McMillan had returned to the wreck to find the others missing so set out once again and this time stumbled across the home of the May family. One of the sons rode across to the Cape Borda lighthouse with news of the disaster and a search party sent out found the other two still struggling towards safety. The third member left behind had not survived.

The steam tug *Euro* was despatched from Adelaide to make a search from the sea. All it found were the remains of the *Loch Sloy* and nine battered bodies washed ashore. Searchers along the beaches found other bodies including the master Captain Nicol and all were buried nearby.

At auction the ship's hull and cargo brought £37, however salvage operations were not particularly successful.

The *Loch Sloy* was an iron ship of 1280 tons, built at Glasgow, Scotland in 1811 on dimensions of 225.3 x 35.6 x 21.2ft for the Glasgow Shipping Line.

The schooner *Maid of Australia,* 45 tons, loaded with flux, and heading for Port Pirie went ashore on the western side of Wardang Island on 8 July and became a total loss.

The schooner *Lucretia* was thrown on to a reef off Spilsby Island in the early hours of 10 September, but the crew of five reached safety. Attempts to refloat the *Lucretia* were frustrated by bad weather and she had to be abandoned. Built in 1885, she was a wooden vessel of 67 tons.

The ketch *Young Surveyor,* on her way to Port Adelaide with a cargo of mallee roots sprang a leak on 2 November and sank. The crew were eventually picked up by a passing vessel. Built in 1811, the *Young Surveyor* was a wooden vessel of 23 tons.

1900

After leaving Scales Bay for Port Adelaide, the schooner *Vale* experienced fine weather until she approached Kangaroo Island when heavy seas caused her to develop a serious leak. Some of her cargo of wheat was jettisoned and Captain Anderson decided to attempt to beach her on Wedge Island, but the water gained so rapidly she was eventually abandoned when about eight miles north-west of Cape Borda. The crew landed safely on Wedge Island and, after remaining for a few days, set out for Edithburgh, being picked up en route by *S.S.Argyle.* Built in 1876 of length 76ft; beam 18.9ft; depth 7ft.

The *Glenpark* left Port Germain for Guam on 28 January with 28,846 bags of wheat (3260 tons) consigned for Algoa Bay in South Africa, then in the early hours of 1 February struck a rock about six kilometres off Wedge Island and sank rapidly, leaving the crew little time to escape. Eventually the barque *Elda* picked them up, then landed them at Port Victoria. Built at Glasgow in 1897, the *Glenpark* was a steel ship of 1959 tons on dimensions of 265.8 x 40 x 23.6ft. Her master was Captain H. Griffiths.

The barge *Gwydir,* loaded with wheat, foundered in Spencer Gulf north west of Tiparra Light while under tow to the tug *Eleanor,* and three lives were lost. Built in 1817, the *Gwydir* was a vessel of 161 tons.

1902

The unregistered cutter *Lord Roberts* was forced ashore near the Myponga jetty by a squall on 1 June.

The cutter *Young Recruit* foundered at Port Gawler on 4 November.

ESCAPE OF THE *DUNCOW*.

(Authors Collection).

The fully rigged sailing ship *Duncow,* 1115 tons, was lucky to escape disaster off Kangaroo Island late in May 1897, on her way from Puget Sound, U.S.A. to Port Pirie with 1,200,000 super-feet of mining timber.

On the evening of the 25th in worsening weather conditions, land loomed up ahead, and after anchors were dropped to hold the ship, a gale raged throughout the night threatening to force her ashore. Next morning she was seen to be lying about 100 metres off shore, below the precipitious cliffs of Cape du Couedic, and during futile attempts to work her off shore she drifted closer in until her stern lay in the breakers.

Eventually, the master decided to abandon his ship and the lifeboat was launched, then rowed to shelter between the Casuarina Islet where it remained for several hours before the crew set out to to safety.

On the 29th, after rowing for 24 hours, a landing was made on the less hostile north west coast of the island and word of the narrow escape of the crew was sent to Adelaide. The tug *Yatala* was immediately sent to the scene with the *Duncow's* crew on board although everyone expected only to find her battered remains. To their surprise the *Duncow* still rode at anchor and after a battle against the sea her crew were placed back on board.

After towing her clear the *Yatala* took her on past Cape Borda to Port Pirie which was reached on 5 June.

Many present day visitors to Cape du Couedic stand on the cliff edge and gaze with awe down the almost sheer cliff at the remains of the ropeway and landing stage, once used to land lighthouse supplies. It was near here that the ship *Duncow* narrowly escaped destruction in 1897. (Author's Collection).

1903

The brigantine *Annie Brown* had called at Spilsby Island in the Sir Joseph Banks Group to load guano on 23 January when a gale drove her ashore without loss of life. Built in 1867, she was a wooden vessel of 160 tons.

The ketch *Eliza*, 29 tons, was lost north of Point Riley near Wallaroo on 29 June.

The wooden ketch *Osprey*, 38 tons, disappeared after leaving Edithburgh on 11 September.

The fishing boat *Enchantress*, 22 tons, stranded at Port Adelaide on 19 September and went to pieces.

The wooden steamer *Eva*, 8 tons, was lost near Cape Willoughby in September.

The barge *Ewbank* was reported lost at Kangaroo Island.

The *Waterlily*, a schooner constructed from one of the twin hulls of the Murray River paddle steamer *Bunyip* sank off Point Malcolm in Lake Alexandrina.

1904

ETHEL

The barque *Ethel* shortly after going ashore near Cape Spencer, 1904.

Bound from South African ports to Semaphore in ballast, the barque *Ethel* went ashore on Reef Head, close to Cape Spencer on the night of 2 January. One member of the crew who attempted to swim ashore with a line lost his hold and was drowned, but the remainder of the crew reached safety.

The wreck was first reported by *S.S.Ferret,* employed in the Port Adelaide-Spencer Gulf trade, when she arrived at Port Adelaide on 4 January. Attempts to free the *Ethel* failed and she became a total loss. Ironically, the *Ferret* was lost only a few metres away seventeen years later and the hulk of the *Ethel* was used to secure a lifeline to rescue the crew.

Built at Sunderland in 1876 the *Ethel* was a three-masted iron barque of 711 tons on dimensions of 177.4 x 30.7 x 18.5ft, and was owned by Norwegian interests.

View on board the wrecked barque *Ethel,* looking forward soon after her loss.

View of the *Ethel* from the cliffs, shortly before she totally broke up in the 1980's.
(Author's Collection).

Captain Lemschow, a well known coastal skipper, led an eventful life at sea and was involved in a number of incidents, the best known being the loss of the *S.S.Napier* at Port Campbell in Victoria, during the salvage work on the *Loch Ard*. The steam tug *Acis*, under his command, went ashore west of Port MacDonnell on 31 January but was not in any immediate danger.

The lifeboat was called with gear in an attempt to refloat her, but when this failed and the weather worsened the *Acis* soon broke up.

Built in 1876, of 27 tons gross, 18 tons net. Length 59.9ft; beam 13ft; depth 6ft.

The barge *Miriam*, 99 tons was lost a Goolwa in February.

The wooden ketch *Ruby*, 20 tons, was lost on Kangaroo Island during November.

1905

The wooden ketch *Britannia*, 34 tons, built in 1896, was wrecked in Spencer Gulf during June.

The 16 ton fishing cutter *Mermaid* was lost near Kangaroo Island during September.

The loss of the schooner *Cygnet* off the northern coast of Kangaroo Island in August cost four lives. She left Port Adelaide for Port Victoria on 5 August, but failed to arrive. A few days later wreckage was sighted in Investigator Strait and the remains of the schooner were eventually located a few miles off shore. The bodies of those drowned were never found.

1906

The fishing cutter *Wanderer*, 11 tons, disappeared off Kangaroo Island on 5 April.

The schooner *New Arrival*, 24 tons, built at Portland in 1875 stranded at Wallaroo on 26 June and became a total loss.

The *Montebello*, a steel barque, was sailing from Hobart to Port Pirie to load wheat when she ran into rough, misty weather and at 2 a.m. on the morning of 18 November and was forced ashore on the south coast of Kangaroo Island. Daylight revealed the shore about one hundred yards away, and after several failures a man succeeded in swimming ashore with a line. All the crew eventually reached the beach where they decided to split into two parties to seek help. All reached safety, but the barque was soon reduced to a total wreck.

Built 1900, of 2284 tons. Length 276.8ft; beam 40.3ft; depth 22.5ft.

The *Columbia* left Wallaroo for Falmouth loaded with wheat but failed to reach her destination. She was a wooden barque of 1381 tons, built in 1871 on dimensions of 205.9 x 40 x 24ft.

The barque *Montebello*, a total wreck near Stunsail Boom River on Kangaroo Island, November 1904.
(Adelaide Observer).

1907

The *Mary Ellis* became a total wreck at Sleaford Bay about 30 kilometres from Port Lincoln on 6 April after being dismasted in a gale during a voyage from Port Adelaide to Venus Bay with a cargo of superphosphate and general items.

She ran into the bay under jury rig to shelter from the gale but after one anchor parted the second was slipped and she was beached. Captain Neuman, four crewmen and a passenger all reached safety.

Built in 1868 she was a wooden ketch of 89 tons on dimensions of 54.8 x 14.8 x 6.1ft.

From Newcastle to Port Pirie with coal, the *Willyama* struck a rock at Rhino Head in Marion Bay on the Yorke Peninsula on 13 April. A tug, with three lighters and a diver attempted to free her but rough weather damaged her so badly she was abandoned.

The *Willyama* was a steel steamer of 2705 tons, built in 1897 on dimensions of 325.5 x 45.1 x 21ft. She was owned by the Adelaide Steam Ship Company.

The steamer *Willyama* on a reef a short distance off shore near Marion Bay on the Yorke Peninsula, 1907. (Author's Collection).

The *Willyama* lies just below the surface with part of her steering mechanism visible. (Peter Christopher).

The cutter **Wanderer** was lost in the Backstairs Passage.

On the morning of 21 April as the four masted barque *Norma* lay at anchor off Semaphore preparing to sail for Europe with a cargo of grain, she was rammed amidships on the port side by the four-masted barque *Ardencraig*, inward bound to Port Adelaide from England with general cargo. The *Norma* sank immediately drowning one of her crew, and she lay submerged only a few metres below the surface. At daylight the 289 ton *Jessie Darling*, inward bound to Port Adelaide passed over the top of the sunken *Norma* and one of her spars ripped through the steamer's bottom, leaving the crew barely time to escape before she sank squarely on top of the sunken wreck.

On the following morning *S.S.Palmer,* running to Adelaide from the stranded *Willyama* also struck the wreck and narrowly escaped disaster. While plans were under way to salvage the *Norma's* cargo the *S.S.Port Chalmers* also struck her and was holed. During the first week of January 1908 the *Jessie Darling* was raised, and following repairs resumed trading, but attempts to raise the *Norma* failed and after several years the remains were removed by dynamite.

Built in 1893 the *Norma* was a steel four-masted barque of 2122 tons on dimensions of 278 x 41.2 x 24.1ft.

The schooner *Post Boy,* 62 tons was built at Port Adelaide in 1874 for trade in local waters. In December 1816 she foundered in St. Vincents Gulf about eleven kilometres west of Glenelg with the loss of six lives, then was raised, repaired and returned to service. In 1895, she went ashore at Port Minlacowie, northeast of Point Turton in Spencer Gulf but was refloated. Her register closed in 1907 with "wrecked" this final time apparently in Arno Bay on the western shores of Spencer Gulf.

The *Aagot* became the first overseas vessel to be destroyed on Wardang Island, after leaving Semaphore on 11 October to load wheat at Port Victoria. She entered Spencer Gulf in a southerly gale and was forced on to rocks on the island's western side, where she was soon a total wreck with her main and foremast over the side, and a heavy list.

Rough seas imprisoned the crew on board until the ebb tide moderated conditions and allowed a member of the crew to swim ashore with line. After reaching the shore the crew used one of the ship's boats to cross to Port Victoria.

Built at Glasgow in 1882 as the *Firth Of Clyde,* she was an iron barque of 1242 tons on dimensions of 228 x 36 x 21ft. She was owned by Norwegian interests when lost.

1908

The motor launch *Triton* was burnt off Point Victor on 12 January.

The wooden ketch *Sir Wilfred Lawson,* 41 tons, was lost near Point Moorowie on 20 March.

The wooden ketch *Triumph,* 19 tons, foundered somewhere between the Yorke Peninsula and Adelaide around 17 September.

S.S.Ellen went ashore at Morgan's Beach about one and a half miles north of Cape Jervis on 12 December and became a total loss. Built 1883, 91 tons gross, 62 tons net. Length 95.3ft; beam 18.6ft; depth 5.7ft.

The wooden schooner *Robert Burns* loaded with copper ore and timber went ashore in Nepean Bay, Kangaroo Island, in December and became a total loss. Built 1857, of 45 tons. Dim: 66.7 x 17.4 x 6.8ft.

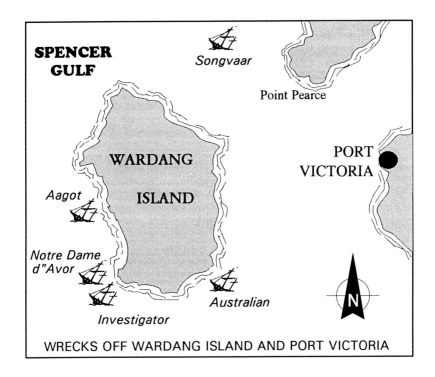

WRECKS OFF WARDANG ISLAND AND PORT VICTORIA

1909

Loaded with bagged wheat and flour, the *Clan Ranald* left Port Adelaide for South African ports on 30 January. Next day, when off the Yorke Peninsula the wind freshened from the south east, and in rough seas the vessel listed sharply to starboard. The rudder was put hard over to bring her head into the wind and sea but she failed to respond and commenced to drift towards the coast. An anchor was dropped but the list increased and eventually the *Clan Ranald* rolled over and sank, taking with her six Europeans including the master, Captain Gladston, and thirty-four Asiatics.

During the inquiry into the tragedy it was disclosed that two fires had broken out in the coal bunkers during loading and had been extinguished using water from the fire hoses. About 170 tons of coal had been removed from the bunkers and stored on deck afterwards. This remained when she sailed and could have made her top heavy. Like twenty-six other Clan Line steamers, she was a turret decked vessel built for the carriage of bulk cargoes. Instead of her sides being straight from the waterline to the bulwarks, they curved inwards about midway up, giving her a ledge or shoulder about three metres below the bulwarks where the breadth was about six metres less than the hull where the inward curve began on both sides.

The *Aagot* ashore off Wardang Island, October 1907. She soon broke up.
(State Library of South Australia, 1979).

Portholes recovered from the *Aagot,* now in the port Victoria Museum.
(Photo courtesy Stuart Moody).

Anchor from the steamer *Clan Ranald* set up on the foreshore at Troubridge Hill on the Yorke Peninsula, near where she foundered in 1909. (Author's Collection).

The rounded hull and large hatchways allowed the ship to be easily filled. Above the turret deck the hull structure ran fore and aft and was called the harbour deck. It was not flat, but shoulder shaped, and a protecting chain threaded through stanchions ran along its edge. It could not be used safely except in port.

Built at Sunderland in 1900, the *Clan Ranald* was 3596 tons on dimensions of 355 x 45.6 x 24.7ft, registered at Glasgow. The ship is protected under the Historic Shipwreck Act.

The *Monarch* went ashore about a kilometre west of Cliff Point, Wardang Island on 1 April during a voyage from Port Victoria to Warrens Beach, where she soon filled with water and broke up.

Built in 1871 she was a three-masted wooden schooner of 132 tons on dimensions of 109 x 33.9 x 7.6ft.

The *Dianella,* a well known trader between Port Adelaide and Port Pirie ran ashore in Moonta Bay on 3 October after springing a leak in boisterous weather and heading for shelter after the pumps were unable to contain her. She had on board 258 bales of wool, 50 tons of ironstone and a few general items. Most was salvaged.

Built in 1872, she was a wooden schooner of 84 tons on dimensions of 90 x 19.2 x 8.1ft.

Grave of the officers of the *Clan Ranald* in the Edithburgh Cemetery. The grave of the coloured crew members is unmarked. (Peter Christopher).

S.S.Time, well known in the coastal trade, carrying a cargo of salt struck a reef near Beachport only about a mile from where the *Euro* had been lost thirty years earlier and became a total wreck. She was sailing close inshore in the early hours of 13 January during a strong offshore gale when she struck rocks and was holed. Her distress rockets were unanswered so a boat was launched to seek assistance at Beachport. Two ships, *S.S.Somerset* and *S.S.Kyarra,* stood by the wreck and managed to take off some of the crew until the lifeboat arrived to complete the rescue.

Built 1890, 2575 tons gross; 1670 tons net. Length 300ft; beam 41ft; depth 19.6ft.

The fishing cutter *Brothers* was lost at Cape Cassini, Kangaroo Island on 13 June.

TWICE SHIPWRECKED

(State Library of South Australia).

The crew of the French barque *Jean Bart* had the unusual experience of being shipwrecked twice in a week. On 7 March, 1913, the *Jean Bart,* from Antwerp to Wallaroo with coke stranded on the western side of Wardang Island. She was eventually refloated, but while her crew were awaiting salvage operations, they were transferred to the big French barque *General De Sonis* which had just finished loading at Port Victoria.

On 12 March, during a heavy gale the *General De Sonis* dragged her anchors and went ashore with crews of both vessels still on board.

The *Jean Bart* was eventually refloated, but not before she had been abandoned to the underwriters. Later she was sold to German interests and renamed *Heinz.* After an eventful career she was finally wrecked in the Bristol Channel in October 1916.

The *General De Sonis* was also refloated after most of her cargo had been unloaded into a lighter. She visited Saigon, Geelong, San Francisco, then completed several voyages to French Guiana and the West Indies before being broken up at Bruges in 1932.

The remains of the *Margit* are still clearly visible in the sand on the Coorong.
She was wrecked in 1911.
(Author's Collection).

The desolate sandy beach of the Coorong quickly claimed the three-masted iron barque *Margit* when she ran ashore about thirty-four miles north of Kingston on 10 November. The *Margit* loaded 23,835 bags of wheat at Victor Harbour but a few days before she was due to sail for the United Kingdom, her master disappeared. He left the ship early one morning to secure a pilot earlier than had been arranged, but he was not seen again, his boat being found bottom up on the beach. After some delay a new master was appointed and the ship sailed, only to run ashore on the same day.

When she struck, heavy seas swept over her forcing the crew into one lifeboat. She lay in the surf with sails flapping noisily in the wind, while the crew hung astern of her throughout the night. At dawn they returned on board but lost the ship's papers when heavy seas crushed the boat. Then, using rocket equipment they landed safely before the rocket crew and lifeboat arrived from Kingston.

The *Margit* was abandoned to the underwriters who sold her for £211 to a salvage company confident she could be refloated. Work was progressing favourably when tragedy struck. Two men, working near the pumps were overcome by fumes from the rotting wheat and lost their lives. Further attempts to refloat the barque failed. She was stripped of all valuable fittings and abandoned.

Built at Londonderry in 1891; 1241 gross tons, 1163 register tons. Length 226ft; beam 36.4ft; depth 21.9ft.

The wooden ketch *Wilpena*, 12 tons, foundered off Port Jarroid on 11 November.

The ketch *Elizabeth Annie*, 64 tons, stranded near the Minlacowie jetty on 16 December and was later abandoned as a total loss.

1912

After arriving at Port Victoria in April, the *Songvaar* was moved to the outer anchorage between Point Pearce and Wardang Island, and 40,707 bags of wheat were taken on board.

In the early hours of the 14th she commenced listing to port and it was discovered that one of her anchors had cut a hole in her hull up forward. The *Songvaar* soon settled on the seabed with her decks awash

The Norwegian owned *Songvaar* on the seabed off Wardang Island after being holed by one of her anchors, April 1912. She could not be raised and was eventually demolished.

TWO LOST FROM LIGHTHOUSE

In the early hours of 17 November 1912, the 1887 ton sailing ship *Dimsdale* struck the Wonga Shoal lighthouse off Semaphore, collapsing it into the sea. Rescuers who hurried to the scene found only a few broken piles standing and the ship at anchor a short distance away. After an extensive search, the bodies of the two lighthouse keepers were recovered, while the master of the *Dimsdale* had his certificate suspended for twelve months. He was also charges with the manslaughter of the two keepers but was acquitted. (Photo: Department of Transport, 1975).

and after several unsuccessful salvage attempts was abandoned in mid May and sold to the Salvage Company of Australia for £210, the cargo of wheat realising a mere £10. As she was a major hazard to other shipping the *Songvaar* was blown up and demolished after capsizing in a gale. Built at Stockton in 1884 as the *Barcore,* she was an iron ship of 2128 tons on dimensions of 278.6 x 40.8 x 24.5ft, and was owned by Norwegian interests.

After leaving Venus Bay for Port Victoria loaded with 3050 bags of wheat, the *Australian* struck a reef on the south eastern corner of Wardang Island on 8 May and was soon a total wreck.

Captain Gustafson and his crew of fifteen rowed safely to Port Victoria after abandoning her, fearing a boiler explosion.

Built at Dundee in 1879 she was an iron schooner rigged steamer of 352 tons on dimensions of 160.3 x 22.5 x 10.5ft. Owned by the West Coast Shipping Company of Port Adelaide.

The *Australian* lies totally wrecked on Wardang island in May 1912.
(Author's Collection).

1913

On the night of 13 March the *Albatross* struck Eclipse Reef near Port Victoria during a heavy gale. Blankets dipped in kerosene and ignited attracted help and all were saved. Built in 1874, she was a wooden ketch of 77 tons on dimensions of 79.3 x 20.2 x 7.1ft.

1914

Twenty-two lives were lost when the iron bucket dredge *Posidonia* vanished in the Great Australian Bight late in January after leaving Port Pirie for Fremantle, Western Australia.

The steamers *Governor Musgrave* and *Penguin* searched the ocean and entire coastline without finding any trace of her. Some believed she may have foundered in rough weather when only about forty kilometres south of Rottnest Island, off Fremantle, Western Australia.

1915

The fishing cutter *Vera* was wrecked near Cape du Couedic, Kangaroo Island on 26 July.

1917

Struck by a violent gale when nearing Kangaroo Island after a voyage from San Francisco with a cargo of timber, the big four-masted schooner *Kona* struck a shoal on the morning of 3 January. Huge seas swept her, but the crew of eleven escaped in a boat shortly before she went to pieces, scattering wreckage and timber over a wide area. Built in 1901, of 679 tons. Length 184ft; beam 38.5ft: depth 14ft.

Remains of the American four-masted schooner *Kona* on the beach, 1917.
(Author's Collection).

The barge *Success*, 49 tons, was lost on the Troubridge Shoal during May .

The wooden ketch *Lillie Hawkins,* 84 tons, built at Port Huon in Tasmania in 1875, carrying 90 tons of superphosphate, dragged her anchors at Port Gibbon in Spencer Gulf on 6 April and went ashore. The crew landed safely.

Lightkeepers on Margaret Brock Reef, off Cape Jaffa received medals from the Royal Humane Society following their rescue of the only two survivors from the lost tug *Nyora*.

The *Nyora* was towing an American schooner from Port Pirie to Sydney when struck by heavy seas. One enormous wave struck the small tug, and she foundered a short time after, about twelve miles off Cape Jaffa, watched by those on the helpless schooner. The first the light keepers knew of the tragedy was twenty-four hours later when they noticed two men in a waterlogged boat about half a mile out to sea.

A fierce wind and rain squall was sweeping the area and the sea was high and confused, but the men did not hesitate. They quickly lowered their sixteen foot dinghy, and after a terrific battle, reached the boat just as it was being dashed to pieces against the rocks, to pluck the captain and a seaman from the jaws of death. Built in 1909, of 309 tons gross, 5 tons net,the *Nyora* was of dimensions 135 x 25.1 x 13.5ft.

The wooden ketch *Ina,* 56 tons, was wrecked on Spilsby Island in Spencer Gulf on 10 November.

In mild weather the steamer *Investigator* went ashore on the south west tip of Wardang Island on 24 April during a voyage from Port Augusta to Port Adelaide via Port Victoria, with two passengers and a cargo of 200 tons of phosphate. With a large hole torn in her side she

The tug *Nyora* which foundered off Cape Jaffa in 1917. (Author's Collection).

soon broke up in the rough weather which developed within a couple of days. The crew and passengers reached Port Victoria in one of the steamer's lifeboats. Owned by the Adelaide Steamship Company, the *Investigator* was an iron steamer of 605 tons, built at Glasgow in 1882 on dimensions of 210.3 x 28.3 x 12.5ft. Her master was T.Gustafsen.

The wooden schooner *Maldon Lewis,* 51 tons, was destroyed by the sea after being beached in Stenhouse Bay on 3 September.

1919

Faulty navigation was blamed for the wreck of the 650 ton steel steamer *Pareoa* on the Althorpe Islands, at about 4 a.m. on 19 September. She left Port Pirie for Hobart with 700 tons of zinc concentrates and apparently grazed a reef about a kilometre west of the islands before striking a rock known locally as The Monument, and was swept by heavy seas and broke up quickly. Among the eleven who lost their lives were the master, Captain McFarlane and the mate J. Booth.

A relief boat was sent from Port Adelaide while the ketch *Broughton* and cutter *Zephr* spearheaded a land and sea search for survivors and those missing. The *Pareoa* had only recently been purchased by the Electrolyt Zinc Company of Australia and had undergone an extensive overhaul at Port Adelaide.

She was built in 1896 for the Canterbury Steam Shipping Company, and named *Breeze.* She was purchased and renamed by the New Zealand Shipping Company in 1900, then sold to W.A. Firth of Sydney in 1911. Her dimensions were 180 x 29.2 x 11.1ft.

The wooden ketch **Young Foster,** 24 tons, foundered near Outer Harbour, Port Adelaide on 21 October.

1920

The wooden cutter **Buck,** 15 tons, foundered near Outer Harbour, Port Adelaide on 2 February.

The magnificent *Notre Dame d'Avor.*

The **Notre Dame d'Avor** was inward bound from Rochefort to Port Victoria in ballast to load wheat when she grounded on the south west corner of Wardang Island at about 10.30p.m. on 20 March. Unfortunately, the light placed on Wardang Island in 1909 was incorrectly marked on the chart and this probably contributed to the wreck.

After unsuccessfully trying to free her the crew of twenty-five left next day on the *S.S.Jessie Darling,* leaving the tugs *Eagle* and *Defiance* to attempt to tow her off after 1400 tons of ballast had been taken out. On the night of 1 May the wreck was gutted by fire after one of the salvage crew accidentally dropped a kerosene lamp, and the resulting fire spread to a store of paint and oils. The burnt-out hulk was later auctioned for £200.

Built at Nantes in 1902, the **Notre Dame d'Avor** was a steel barque of 2646 tons on dimensions of 276.8 x 40.4 x 22.5 feet.

The **Iron Barge No.2** was lost in Spencer Gulf during August.

In 1904 when the steamer **Ferret** arrived at Port Adelaide after one of her weekly visits to ports in Spencer Gulf her master reported a ship ashore on Reef Head close to Cape Spencer. Closer investigation

Waves sweep over the steamer *Ferret*, ashore on Reef Head, close to Cape Spencer, 1904. (SSL:M:B7223).

A lifeline was secured to the wreck of the *Ethel,* and the crew of the *Ferret* were soon safely ashore. (SSL:M:B7224)

identified her as the *Ethel*. By a coincidence the **Ferret** was lost a few metres away on 13 November, and the hulk of the barque was used to secure a line to the steamer. The **Ferret** left Port Adelaide for Port Victoria late in the afternoon, but ran into fog when off the Yorke Peninsula, and after steering too close in shore ran on to the beach where she was battered and holed by heavy seas. The first lifeboat launched capsized in the surf, but the occupants reached shore, and after a lifeline was rigged all twenty-one landed safely. The tug *Euro* was despatched to the scene but was unable to take the crew aboard so they were instructed to make their way overland to Stenhouse Bay where she picked them up.

In 1880-81 the *Ferret* achieved notoriety after being stolen during a voyage from Cardiff to Marsailles. The thieves were eventually arrested at Melbourne and the *Ferret* remained in Australian waters.

Built at Glasgow in 1871, the *Ferret* was an iron steamer of 460 tons on dimensions of 170.9 x 23.2 x 12.7 feet. She was owned by the Adelaide Steam Ship Company and her master was Captain Blair.

The wooden ketch *Lillie May,* 43 tons, foundered off Cape Elizabeth in Spencer Gulf on 6 June with the loss of five lives.

Remains of the *Lemael* on the beach.
(Author's Collection).

The schooner *Lemael,* Captain Holyman, sailing from Tasmania to Adelaide with timber and general cargo, was lost near Cape Banks on 21 July. Terrific gales battered her for days eventually carrying away the mainmast and leaving her helpless to be cast up onto a reef. Two of the seven crew drifted ashore on a plank and set out for help, but the remainder waited until the vessel began to break up before leaving her. All reached safety but suffered badly from exposure. Built in 1892, of 98 tons, on dimensions of 101.7 x 26.3 x 7.7 feet.

1923

The wooden ketch *Trucanini,* 40 tons, was lost near Point Malcolm on 5 January.

The wooden ketch *Morning Star,* 17 tons was lost at Glenelg on 16 November.

128

After being battered by a gale, the schooner *Lemael* was driven ashore and lost near Cape Banks in 1921. (Author's Collection).

1924

Built at Port Adelaide in 1876, the 36 ton wooden ketch *Portonian* traded around the Australian coast until converted into a fishing cutter in 1924. On 26 October she went ashore on Troubridge Island and could not be salvaged.

1925

The schooner *Victor,* 32 tons, was lost on Balgowan Reef during January.

The schooner *Helena,* 24 tons, was lost near Whittelby Point on 4 September.

The ketch *Lialeeta* left Balgowan on 11 April bound for Melbourne but was not seen again after calling at Semaphore for provisions. The vessel carried a crew of five and 112 tons of barley. Built in 1913, of 82 tons gross, 48 tons net. Length 78ft; beam 22.8ft; depth 6.6ft.

The *Lialeeta* was one of the best known sail traders around the southern coastline when she disappeared after leaving Semaphore in 1925. (Author's Collection).

1926

The small steamer *Fairy*, 18 tons, was destroyed by fire at Port Pirie on 9 January.

Beached after developing a leak near Point Turton on 29 May, the wooden steam tug *Yalta* was later abandoned. Built at Nowra in 1877, she was a vessel of 64 tons. She was bought by the Adelaide Steam Tug Company in 1909 when her name was changed from *James Comrie*.

The ketch *Dashing Wave*, 39 tons, was lost in Louth Bay on 25 December.

THEFT OF A STEAMER

(Author's Collection).

When the steamer *Ferret* was wrecked at Reef Head on 13 November 1920, she had already achieved notoriety in her 50 year life, following an international incident in 1880 when the alertness of Melbourne police solved the mystery of her disappearance during a voyage between Glasgow, Scotland and Melbourne, resulting in a prison sentence for three men accused of her theft.

The *Ferret,* owned by the Railway Company of Scotland, was chartered in September and left ostensibly for Marseilles. However, after passing Gibraltar a boat and life belts were thrown overboard, her colours and name changed, then she sailed into hiding in the Atlantic and then on to South America. She disposed of her cargo at Cape Town and Mauritius then set course for Australia.

When she arrived at Albany in Western Australia bearing the name *India,* she was already being viewed with suspicion as her owners had notified Lloyds and the Board of Trade of the suspicious circumstances surrounding her disappearance.

Then as she passed through Port Phillip Heads on April 20th, 1881, word was telegraphed to Melbourne placing the authorities on the alert. Customs and Health officials who boarded her appeared satisfied but when those on board opened negotiations for her sale the police moved in.

Examination of her papers revealed false logbooks, stamps and also seals and dies of different countries. The guilt of those on board was proved beyond doubt and they were convicted.

The *Ferret* was purchased by W.Whinham who ran her in the South East of South Australia trade, then sold her to the Adelaide Steamship Company in 1883. They refitted her then she was placed in the Western Australia trade. She also ran on the South Australian west coast and was operating around the Yorke Peninsula when lost.

In 1888, *Ferret* was one of the first steamers to carry silver and lead mined at Broken Hill, from Port Pirie to Adelaide.

During the seamens' strike in 1893, the Adelaide Steamship Company employed a number of outsiders to crew their vessels. There was trouble on the *Ferret* when one of the "scratch" hands was knocked off the wharf at Wallaroo while helping to ship a horse and was severely injured, spending more than five weeks in hospital.

1927

While sailing in gusty conditions from Port Victoria to Wallaroo with wheat, the schooner *Macintyre* got into difficulties off the southern end of Wardang Island and ran on to a reef at about midnight on 1 April. Built at Echuca in 1877 as a river boat and later converted to a steamer at Port Adelaide, she was a vessel of 127 tons measuring 109.8 x 21 x 7.5 feet.

Wreck of the auxiliary schooner *MacIntyre* on Wardang Island. (Author's Collection).

While sheltering from a gale in Port le Hunte, the ketch *Spindrift* dragged her anchors and went ashore. Captain Brown and the crew of three reached safety. Built in 1873 she was a wooden vessel of 71 tons measuring 79.6 x 21.6 x 6.9 feet.

On 19 August the wooden auxiliary schooner *Rooganah* was carrying a general cargo which included cases of benzine into Whyalla when her petrol engine backfired and set her alight . The crew left quickly and she was soon destroyed. Built in 1909 the *Rooganah* was a vessel of 99 tons, measuring 95 x 25.1 x 7 feet.

1928

The auxiliary two-masted schooner *Four Winds,* 21 tons, was burnt off Port Adelaide on 1 March.

Early in April the 46 ton ketch *Ariel* disappeared with her crew of three off the Althorpe Islands, and wreckage was later found near Cape Doningham.

1929

The ketch *Merle* was burnt at Port Adelaide on 2 January.

The wooden auxiliary schooner *Eclipse,* 79 tons, built at Footscray in 1864 was wrecked on Wolff Reef in Spencer Gulf on 30 April.

1930

The schooner *Eleanor* was laden with wheat when lost on a reef off the Sir Joseph Banks Group of Islands on 18 February while bound from Port Neill to Port Lincoln. Built as an iron paddle steamer and converted to a three masted schooner, she was a vessel of 116 tons on dimensions of 130.3 x 20.2 x 101.1 feet.

1932

The auxiliary ketch *Vivid,* 45 tons, disappeared between Tumby Bay and Port Lincoln in April, with a crew of three and 1000 bags of wheat.

The steel, four masted barque *Hougomont* was dismasted when about 800 kilometres south of Cape Borda on the night of 20 April and limped into Port Adelaide nineteen days later, where she was condemned, then towed around to Stenhouse Bay and sunk there as a breakwater for the Waratah Gypsum Company. Built at Greenock in 1897 the *Hougomont* was a vessel of 2428 tons, measuring 292.4 x 43.2 x 24 feet.

After springing a leak near Dashwood Bay on Kangaroo Island the cutter *Vectis* was run ashore on 8 August. Salvage attempts were unsuccessful.

The 28 ton cutter *Minnie Sims* was sheltering at Cape Willoughby, Kangaroo Island when her anchor chain parted and she went ashore and soon broke up. No lives were lost.

The dismasted *Hougomont* limps into Port Adelaide, May 1932.
(Author's Collection).

After being condemned, the *Hougomont* was towed around to Stenhouse Bay
and sunk there as a breakwater for the Waratah Gypsum Company.
(George Leggett Collection).

The Danish motor ship *Victoria* on the way to Wallaroo with 6,300
tons of phosphate from Makatea ran off course in Backstairs Passage
and struck rocks near Porpoise Head about six miles east of Cape
Jervis.

She lay about fifty metres off shore with about five metres of water in her forepeak and was leaking badly. Three tugs despatched from Port Adelaide failed to refloat her so a line was fastened ashore and the vessel abandoned. Salvage crews often worked in rough conditions to remove fittings from the vessel which eventually broke her back and went to pieces before work on her was completed.

Built in 1928, she was a twin screw steamer of 4,500 tons gross. Length 384ft; beam 54ft; depth 24ft.

After tugs failed to free *M.V.Victoria,* ashore near Cape Jervis in 1934, salvage crews were working to remove fittings when she broke in two and quickly went to pieces. (SSL:M:B6530).

All that remained of the *Victoria* in 1949. (Author's Collection).

A COLOURFUL VETERAN

After a few years service as a breakwater for the Waratah Gypsum Company at Stenhouse Bay, the hulk of the old four masted steel barque *Hougomont* soon broke up and disappeared; and apart from her Finnish owners, there were few who remembered much of her thirty-five year eventful career, or cared enough to mourn her shameful demise.

Built in 1897 for John Hardie of Glasgow, the *Hougomont* was a low sided, heavily rigged vessel, designed for the fierce winds of the high latitudes, which made for several fast voyages, particularly in her early years.

She attracted notice with her first major mishap in February 1903, as she completed a voyage from San Francisco to Liverpool with a capacity cargo of wheat, barley, canned fruit and salmon. A tug took her in tow in a heavy gale but the line parted and she was driven on to the beach at Allonby Bay. Dismasted, and with heavy seas breaking over her and dislodging the cargo most believed she would be lost, yet within a month she was refloated and eventually returned to service.

In July 1908, during a short voyage in ballast between the South American ports of Coquimbo and Tocopilla, expected to take five days, she disappeared and three months later arrived unexpectedly at Sydney, more than 6000 nautical miles from her planned destination. Adverse winds had caused this remarkable voyage. Next, in 1914, she stranded on Fire Island near New York in a dense fog but was refloated without much trouble.

John Hardie sold her to the famous Captain Erikson in 1924, and from 1926 she was seen regularly in Australian waters. While outward bound to Melbourne in 1928 she was dismasted in the North Atlantic but was towed to Lisbon and refitted.

The *Hougomont* loaded wheat at Port Lincoln in 1929 and Wallaroo in 1931, then was returning to load again at a South Australian port in 1932 when disaster struck south of Cape Borda.

1935

The *Portland Maru* loaded grain at Port Pirie and set out for home, despite a slight list apparently caused by faulty loading. She called at Port Lincoln, where she was examined by divers, but her master decided to proceed. When off Kangaroo Island she apparently struck an unidentified object, and began to settle in the bow as she headed back towards Port Adelaide for repairs.

It soon became obvious she would not reach port so ships stood by until she was beached a short distance to the west of Cape Torrens, where she was swept by moderate seas. The crew were eventually transferred to the tug *Wato* and within a few days the steamer commenced to break up.

Built 1919. 5865 tons. Length 385 feet; beam 51 feet; depth 36 feet.

1937

The 50 ton auxiliary ketch *Heather Belle* was destroyed by fire at Wallaroo on 15 May.

The cutter *Rapid* was lost on the Althorpe Islands on 19 September.

The cutter *Albatross* was lost at Wedge Island on 20 October.

Built in 1907 as a lighthouse inspection vessel, then used as a yacht, the 24 ton ketch *Stormy Petrel* was fishing near Cape Cassini on Kangaroo Island on 21 December when she struck a reef and was lost.

1938

The fishing boat *Janet* was lost while crayfishing near Cape Cassini on Kangaroo Island.

The fishing cutter *Stella* was also lost on Kangaroo Island. She was swept on to rocks near Cape du Couedic on 8 May.

The motor launch *Glenelg* was lost at Rapid Bay during June.

1939

The tug *Robbie Burns* was lost near Corny Point.

The cutter *Elsie* was lost near Carrickalinga.

The *Vixen* sank off Droughty Point on 27 November drowning one of her crew.

1942

The cray boat *Winnie* was run ashore in West Bay, Kangaroo Island on 7 January after being damaged by heavy seas.

The 46 ton ketch *Free Selector* was wrecked at Outer Harbour, Port Adelaide on 5 September.

The Adelaide Steam Ship Company chartered *S.S.Kapara* to Coast Steamships Limited after their *S.S.Yandra* had been requisitioned by the Australian Navy, and she continued the service from Adelaide to the Eyre Peninsula. In the early hours of 13 November, in calm hazy conditions she ran on to a reef off the south eastern corner of Flinders Island and was badly holed. At daylight the crew abandoned her and her remains were sold in January 1943.

Built at Sunderland in 1914, the *Kapara* was a steel steamer of 846 tons, measuring 195 x 32.1 x 12.5 feet.

In the early days shallow draughted sail traders with retractable centre boards, like the ketch *Free Selector* (pictured), used this method to unload cargo at many remote South Australian ports. (Kingscote Museum).

The *Kapara* lies a total wreck. (State Library of South Australia).

138

THE WAR AT SEA

Although enemy surface raiders and submarines made several incursions into South Australian waters during World War 2, the damage they inflicted was relatively light compared with some other sections of the Australian coast.

In 1940 the German raider *Pinguin* laid mines at the entrance to Spencer Gulf and on 7 December the British freighter *Hertford* was badly damaged by one of these. After temporary repairs at Port Lincoln she was eventually towed to Adelaide for further repairs. Permanent hull repairs were completed at Sydney on 24 November, 1941, almost a year after she was mined. The ship was not ready for sea until 20 January 1942, all to no avail as she was torpedoed and lost on her homeward voyage to England on 29 March 1942.

In another incident, this time in 1944, the steamer *Illossis* was shelled by the German submarine U.862 when off Kingston, but she escaped when the approach of an Australian aircraft forced the submarine to dive.

1943

While crayfishing off Kangaroo Island, the cutter *Stormbird* struck rocks, was run ashore, then abandoned .

1946

The cutter *Venus* was lost on North Neptune Island on 14 June.

The ketch *Lurline* was well known for many years around the South Australian coast where she engaged in coastal trading and fishing. Schooner rigged, in later years she also carried an auxiliary engine and a small lifeboat. In 1898 she was driven ashore near Beachport but the crew reached safety and she was eventually refloated.

In March 1946 she left for Melbourne manned by her new owner, R. O'Toole, his son and one other, but was disabled by a squall. She anchored in Rapid Bay for repairs but, after getting under way again struck trouble and after dragging her anchors for several miles, went ashore on Sellick's Beach. Some equipment was salvaged, but she soon became a total wreck.

Built 1813. 59 tons. Length 19 feet; beam 18.5 feet; depth 7.1 feet.

The 32 ton ketch *Cecelia* was wrecked at Port le Hunte on 4 October after dragging her anchors and going ashore.

The ketch *Lurline*, stranded at Beachport in 1898, the finally wrecked in Rapid Bay in 1946.
(Author's Collection).

1947

In heavy seas the 49 ton ketch **Broughton** dragged her anchors and went ashore at Flint Point near Port MacDonnell on 14 July. The lifeboat, and a dinghy manned by the son of the lighthouse keeper rescued the crew of three.

1948

A severe gale destroyed the cutters **Renown** and **Zephyr** at Glenelg on 11 April.

In winds gusting up to 80 knots, three shark fishing boats were destroyed at Robe on 29 May. They were the 30 ft **Ebor, Jennifer,** 45 ft and **La Paloma,** 45 ft.

The cutter **Tarna** was believed lost off the Yorke Peninsula during June.

The fishing ketch **Miss Echo** was lost at Victor Harbour.

140

Three fishing vessels were lost in a big storm at Robe, 1948.
(Robe Library and Information Centre).

ANOTHER CLOSE CALL

Stories of strandings, fires and other near disasters off the South Australian coast through more than 150 years would fill many volumes, particularly incidents in the days of sail. In recent times comparatively few large ships have been seriously threatened, but the ex Liberty Ship *Mill Hill,* 7210 tons was lucky to escape becoming a total loss in August 1950 after her cargo of pig iron shifted in heavy weather when she was off the far west coast and she developed a dangerous list.

On 20 August the crew abandoned her off Cape Radstock, and the Huddart Parker tug *Foremost* began the hazardous tow to safety. Barely able to control the lifeless hulk she called the South Australian Harbours Board tug *Tancred* in to help and Port Lincoln was reached on the 25th.

Built as the *Sameden* in 1944 the vessel was renamed *Mill Hill* in 1947; *Educator* in 1951; *Kanaris* in 1961; *Splendid Sky* in 1966. She was broken up in Belgium in 1970 after being badly damaged when she ran aground near Antwerp.

1951

On 26 February, during a heavy fog, the freighter **Corio** ran on to Carpenter Reef only a short distance from where the *Admella* had been lost eighty years earlier. She was only little more than a quarter of a mile offshore and nothing could be done to save her. The *Iron Yampi* took off her crew, and the vessel eventually broke her back, becoming a total wreck.

Built in 1919, of 3346 tons gross, 1934 tons net. Length 331 feet; beam 41.9 feet; depth 23.6 feet.

The fishing boat *May* went ashore near Cape Willoughby on Kangaroo Island on 10 March.

While sailing from Adelaide to the mouth of the Murray River where she was to be converted into a river boat, the 35 ton ketch *Mary* was swept ashore on Kangaroo Island on 1 August.

1954

The 51 ton ketch *John Robb* sank about 8 kilometres west of Outer Harbour, Port Adelaide on 24 April after colliding with the tug *Falcon.*

1955

The motor launch *Grelka* was destroyed by an explosion when off Kangaroo Island on 26 January.

S.S. Corio lies wrecked on Carpenter Rocks in 1951 when carrying a cargo of limestone from Rapid Bay to Port Kembla.
(Author's Collection).

1957

The shark boat *Mars* was lost at Weir Cove, Kangaroo Island on 20 July while sheltering from a gale.

1958

The shark boat *Magic* went ashore on Kangaroo Island on 3 April.

The 15 ton fishing boat *Flying Dutchman* was lost off Wedge Island on 20 May.

1959

The fishing boat *Carleen* was lost at Port MacDonnell.

The *Yandra* ran aground in dense fog on a rocky island in the Neptune Group, near the entrance to Spencer Gulf, on 25 January. The crew of twenty-three used a breeches buoy to abandon the vessel, and reached the island safely, leaving her rolling and bumping heavily on the rocks.

The yacht *Iline,* a competitor in the annual Neptune Island yacht race answered a radio call and assisted the lighthouse keeper's rescue of the marooned seamen, while the tug *Tusker* battled rough seas and stiff southerlies to investigate the possibility of saving the stranded steamer. When she could not be refloated salvagers stripped her before she was destroyed by heavy seas about a month later.

Owned by Coast Steamships Ltd., she was a steel motor vessel of 990 tons, built at Copenhagen in 1928 on dimensions of 211.1 x 35.2 x 11.9 feet.

A BRAVE EFFORT

Bravery displayed by Ron Gifford during the loss of the steamer *Yandra* on Neptune Island in 1959 was recognised by the Royal Humane Society of Australia's Silver Medal. He was a seaman on his first voyage on the *Yandra* and volunteered to make the hazardous swim to the shore with a line when the lifeboats could not be used. After three or four attempts to climb on to the rocks he gained a handhold and dragged himself clear of the surf, suffering a back injury and cuts to his hand and body. Securing the breeches buoy line which he had hauled through the surf, he signalled those on the doomed vessel and soon the first survivors were coming ashore.

The coastal freighter *Yandra* fast on the rocks at the Neptune Islands. Heavy seas soon destroyed her.
(SSL:M:B20221. The News S.A. Pty.Ltd.).

Although the 165 ton auxiliary schooner *Milford Crouch* which capsized and sank near Franklin Harbour, Spencer Gulf on 27 October, with the loss of six of her crew, was eventually salvaged and returned to service in 1961, the seriousness of the incident warrants its inclusion.

1960

After leaving Robe on 4 November the crayfish cutter *Marco Polo* was not seen again.

1961

The tuna boat *Lincoln Star* disappeared off Rock Island near Port Lincoln on 27 February, taking seven lives.

The fishing boat *Marleesh* was lost near Robe.

The fishing boat *Florence* was lost off the Eyre Peninsula.

1962

The fishing boat *Cookaburra* was wrecked in Emu Bay, Kangaroo Island on 19 May.

1963

The tuna boat *Smada* foundered south of Port Lincoln on 7 February.

While sheltering from a storm off Kangaroo Island on 18 March, the anchor of the fishing cutter *Joan Margaret* parted and she went ashore.

The cutter *Kookaburra* was lost near Cape Borda on 16 April. Two men lost their lives and wreckage came ashore near the Ravine des Casoars.

1964

The trawler *Leprena* was destroyed by fire off Point Moorowie on the Yorke Peninsula on 12 February. Built in 1912 as the *Forbes Brothers,* she was vessel of 109 tons.

The launch *Mariner* was wrecked at Rapid Bay on 21 July.

The fishing boat *Thunderbird* was lost at Cape Jaffa on 10 December.

1965

During January the fishing boat *Susanna* sank near Memory Cove while under tow to Port Lincoln.

The fishing boat *Saint Michele* was wrecked on South Neptune Island on 30 March.

The fishing boat *Pelamis* sank near Liguanea Island on 28 April.

1966

The fishing cutter *Jeanette S.* was crayfishing when she foundered off West Bay, Kangaroo Island on 28 April.

The ex-Liberty ship *Eleni K.* lies with her back broken near Goat Island, 1966. (I.G.Stewart).

The cray boat *Miss Jeanette* was lost off Kangaroo Island.

Three officers spent two miserable nights on the freighter *Eleni K,* loaded with 1500 tons of bulk wheat, valued at £435,000, after she broke her back and settled in about eight metres of water about nine kilometres off Ceduna, shortly after leaving Thevenard for the United Kingdom on 29 September. The remaining 27 Greek and Spanish seamen on board had been taken ashore.

On 17 November the vessel was refloated and beached near Goat Island where she was declared a total wreck. Experts who examined her believed an apparent weakness in the vicinity of No.3 hold amidships had caused her to break almost in two.

She was a Liberty Ship of 7245 tons built at Baltimore U.S.A. in 1943 on dimensions of 441.5 x 57.1 x 27.9 feet, and originally named *John Hopkins,* then *Thetis* in 1946, *Sanita Elena* in 1952, and *Elini K* in 1960. She was owned by the Greek Elini Shipping Company when lost.

After being swamped by a freak wave, the cray boat *Alancia* foundered between Carpenter Rocks and Port MacDonnell during November.

1967

When the fishing trawler *Glen Morry* hit rocks and sank off Port Lincoln on 10 June, her crew of four were rescued from life rafts some hours later by *S.S.Dinjerra.*

The trawler *Veronica* went missing between Port MacDonnell and Portarlington during July.

The fishing boat *Heather Christine* was lost near Grey during November.

TO BE TAKEN WITH A GRAIN OF SALT

The lore of the sea is crammed with tales spawned in the era of the ancient navigators and the "Great Days of Sail ." Not often does the mystery surrounding a modern day incident provide the opportunity for the maritime story teller to exercise his imagination, thus paving the way for what may one day in the distant future develop into a fabled sea legend, becoming more coloured with each telling.

Recently, Ron Arbon, an honorary maritime consultant to the State Library of South Australia, recalled a story concerning the loss of the ex-Liberty Ship *Eleni K.* near Thevenard in 1966, passed on to him by that indomitable researcher of South Australian shipwrecks, Ron Temme, who was told the story by a Ceduna resident some years earlier.

Shortly after the *Eleni K.* arrived at Thevenard in September to load wheat, it was declared unseaworthy after waterside workers reported seeing daylight through the hull. She then steamed to Adelaide for repairs to bulkheads and other fittings.

The vessel left Port Adelaide on 22 September to return to Thevenard to load, and a popular story circulating at the time said that wheat was deliberately loaded only in the fore and aft holds to place an excessive strain on the vessel, causing her to break in half in sheltered waters before she faced the open sea.

The all welded construction of the American Liberty Ships had exposed many weaknesses in the ageing hulls, causing a number to break in two and sink, and this may have given rise to rumours regarding the *Eleni K.*

Shortly after the wreck and its cargo was abandoned, Ron Temme flew over the site but could see no sign of the ship. Locals told him it had been stripped by vandals, and the cargo removed by farmers before it disappeared.

How much credence can one place in the story? Often, after a period of time, when facts become distorted, stories like this provide interesting tales to be told for years in hotel bars and places where sea-lovers congregate, before becoming another local saga of the sea.

1968

The tuna boat *Naracoopa* was lost by fire off Cape Bolingbroke on 25 June after an explosion in the engine room which forced the crew of three to abandon her. She was a vessel of 294 tons, built in 1940 on dimensions of 120.4 x 26 x 8.4 feet and used as a coastal trader for many years.

The *Silver Gull* sank during November while crossing the Murray River bar.

Two unnamed fishing boats were lost on the west coast at Spencer Gulf and Coffin Bay.

1969

The fishing boat *Neptune* left Grey for Port Fairy in November with a crew of four and disappeared south-east of Cape Banks.

1971

The fishing boat *St.Kevin* sank in about 50 metres while under tow near Point Sinclair.

The fishing cutter *Hirondelle* sank near Reef Head during November .

1973

The *Amber Star* was lost off Kangaroo Island on 14 January.

The fishing trawler *Bitang Terang* struck a rock off Venus Bay on 1 July and became a total loss.

The fishing boat *Penguin* sank near Port Lincoln on 13 August while under tow to *Cape Byron*.

Three lives were lost when the *Cape Jaffa* disappeared after leaving Kingston for Adelaide.

The *Lorraine* was reported lost west of Port Lincoln in November.

1974

The wooden tuna boat *Degel* was lost near Port Lincoln during January.

The fishing boat *Nadgee Ii* was abandoned in St. Vincents Gulf on 12 March after springing a leak during her first voyage. The crew of six were rescued by *M.V.Troubridge*.

The *Helen* was lost near Port Lincoln during March.

The fishing boat *Telstar* was lost off Beachport on 1 November, drowning the owner.

The yacht *Sigrid* was swamped near Port MacDonnell.

1975

After being badly damaged by fire west of Ceduna, the tuna boat *Sea Hawke* was under tow when she sank on 19 January.

The cray boat *Yasmine* capsized and sank while under tow near West Island on 24 March.

The cray boat **Lady Anne** was lost near Port MacDonnell on 24 March.

The *Maria Stella* was lost at Westall Point, Streaky Bay, on 24 April.

The wrecked fishing boat *Saori* lies perched on a ledge below 200 metre cliffs on Wedge Island.   Photo: Jan Stone, 1983)

The fishing boat *Saori* was driven ashore and lost at the foot of 200 metre cliffs on Wedge Island on 3 June.

The prawn boat *Jadran* was burnt near Corny Point on 6 October.,

An explosion and fire destroyed the tuna boat **Roma Star** near Wedge Island on 5 August.

The *Pacific Gull* was burnt off Ceduna on 6 August.

A fire also destroyed the fishing boat **Bona Star** near Port Lincoln on 6 August.

The powered lighter **Moorara,** ex *Echuca* sank off Wardang Island in August while lying almost derelict. Built in 1909 she was a vessel of 100 tons on dimensions of 111 x 21 x 5.3ft.   Used as a Murray River barge until 1930, then converted to an auxiliary schooner before finishing her days as a lighter. When lost she was owned by the Aboriginal Lands Trust and was used occasionally to carry fresh water from Port Victoria to Wardang Island.

The *Moorara* on the bottom. (Photo courtesy Stuart Moody).

The cray boat **Storm Eagle** was lost on 21 November.

The **Mako** caught fire and foundered at Franklin Harbour on 9 December.

1976

The **Taroona** was burnt near Cape Jaffa on 24 February.

The 18 ton cutter **Corona Astron** was lost north east of Cape St. Albans on Kangaroo Island on 3 March.

The cray boat **Flinders Star** caught fire and foundered near Flinders Island on 5 March.

The fishing boat **Aquainita** sank near Wedge Island on 21 June.

While steaming from Kangaroo Island to Adelaide with gypsum, the **Ulonga** sank in St.Vincents Gulf on 6 July. The crew of five were rescued by *S.S.Star Lily,* then transferred to the prawn vessel *Speedewell.* Formerly a Murray River paddle steamer, she was built at Moana, New South Wales in 1910 and was an iron vessel of 119 tons on dimensions of 111.5 x 22 x 6.9 feet. She was converted to an auxiliary ketch in 1949.

The prawn boat *Katey* foundered near Ceduna on 24 September.

The prawn trawler *Aquarius* caught fire and sank in Spencer Gulf on 28 October.

The cray boat *Lindy Lou* ran aground and broke up in Sceace Bay on the West Coast on 2 November.

The cray boat *Florence* broke up on a reef on the West Coast on 3 November.

The prawn trawler *Santa Anna* was lost near Cowell on 11 December.

The Troubridge Shoal lighthouse which warned of one of the major dangers to shipping approaching Adelaide from the west.
(Department of Transport, 1979).

1977

The wooden cray boat *Explorer* was lost near Cape Jaffa on 1 February.

The *Darren Lee* was lost on 26 February.

The cray boat *Gloridia V* was lost on North Neptune Island on 12 March.

The tuna boat *Zadar* began taking water and was abandoned off the West Coast on 27 April.

The fishing boat *Sunbeam* may have been lost around 20 May.

The fishing boat *Tattler* was lost during a gale on 1 June.

The *Mercury Star* was reported as lost on 3 June.

1978

After the fishing boat *Scamp* sank at her moorings at Beachport on 25 March, she was beached, only to be declared a total loss.

The *Lismore Star* was lost on Kangaroo Island on 30 April.

The 85 ton wooden trawler *Estelle Star* burned and sank off Gibbon Point on 15 May. Built in 1927 at Woy Woy, she ran as a ferry in Port Jackson and Western Port before being sold and converted for fishing.

The fishing boat *Nola Too,* a total wreck on Kangaroo Island.
(Author's Collection)

The shark boat *Nola Too* was wrecked in Vivonne Bay , Kangaroo Island on 23 August.

1979

While steaming to assist the disabled cray boat *Westward,* the tuna boat *Latvia* caught fire and had to be abandoned near Port Lincoln on 28 March.

The fishing boat *Adelaide Renown* was lost near Cape de Couedic on Kangaroo Island on 26 April.

The South Australian Fisheries Department patrol boat *Cape Arid* capsized near Kingscote, Kangaroo Island on 12 December, drowning one member of her crew.

The cutter *Sea Spray* was lost off Kangaroo Island.

1980

The *Farid Fares* on fire off the South Australian coast.
(Photograph courtesy of Peter Watkins, Max Farrell and Associates).

On 27 March, in latitude 38 degrees 20 minutes South, longitude 136 degrees 20 minutes East, while on passage from Devonport to Iranian ports, the livestock carrier *Farid Fares* was badly damaged by a fire which broke out in the engine room and spread to the accommodation section. Next day she was abandoned about 160 kilometres off the South Australian coast, then later on, when sighted from the air, was still on fire. The Polish trawler *Denebola* rescued the crew of seventy-two from the lifeboats, but one member of the crew and 40,605 sheep were lost. The tug *Sir Roy Fidge* also hurried to the scene but the ship had sunk.

A Federal Government Inquiry decided that oil spraying from a broken generator supply line had probably ignited and caused the fire.

The *Farid Fares* was a vessel of 8697 tons on dimensions of 478.6 x 64.1 x 26.2 feet. She was built in 1950 as the refrigerated cargo liner *Lions Gate,* then converted to a livestock carrier by her Lebanese owners, Raschid Fares, in 1973.

1981

The tuna fishing boat *Cape Byron,* formerly an R.A.N. lighter, foundered near Rocky Island, Port Lincoln on 26 January.

1982

The shark boat *Savor* was lost east of Cape Gantheaume on 11 June.

1984

The tuna boat *Velebit,* 70 tons, was lost near Point Bell on the West Coast on 11 January.

The tuna boat *Rosalind Star* was lost south of Ceduna on 24 January.

The barge *Master Jack* loaded with a $100,000 beacon built for the Department of Transport, broke away from the tow of the tug *E.H.Price* off Cape Spencer on 8 May and grounded on Emme's Reef. After drifting free it was then taken in tow by the fishing boat *Marian H.*, but after losing the beacon in rough seas the towline parted on 10 May and the barge finished on rocks at Cape Forbin on the north western side of Kangaroo Island.

Built in 1965 as the 452 tonne bucket dredge *H.C.Meyer,* and owned by the South Australian Department of Marine and Harbours.

1985

The cray boat *Sea Hero* sank near Kingston on 6 January.

The fishing boat *Jedda* from Robe, with four aboard disappeared between Kangaroo Island and the mainland about 17 April. Wreckage was recovered near Robe and at the mouth of the Murray River but there was no sign of the crew.

1986

The cray boat *Nelcie* was overwhelmed by a huge wave off Port MacDonnell on 15 March.

The cray boat *Kate* was wrecked in a storm of the north coast of Kangaroo Island with the loss of one life on 1 December.

1981

The fishing boat *Island Girl* sank off Kangaroo Island on 18 February.

1988

The fishing boat *Queen Maria* foundered south of Kangaroo Island on 22 January.

The cray boat *Shannon* was lost off the Eyre Peninsula on 10 May,

The fishing boat *Dalrymple Star* was destroyed by fire off Port Adelaide on 13 July.

1990

The shark boat *Magee Two* was wrecked near Port Lincoln on 8 August.

The fishing boat *Alien Ii* capsized in rough seas in St. Vincents Gulf on 20 November. The crew of two were rescued by the *Anjeliers Gracht*.

The 13 metre cray boat *Bernadene* foundered near Port MacDonnell on 21 November.

The fishing boat *Joliet Percy* was wrecked on Kangaroo Island on 10 December. The crew of four were rescued by flying fox.

1991

The twelve metre yacht *Wavy Street* was gutted by fire at Port Adelaide on 10 January.

The prawn trawler *Andiah* was destroyed by fire off Port Lincoln on 23 May. The crew of three were rescued.

1992

The fishing boat *Turton Star* disappeared off the far west coast with her crew of two on 8 October. Wreckage was later recovered at several points.

APPENDIX A
A FINE FIGUREHEAD

In the mid 1600's British and French men-o-war displayed figureheads of considerable imagination and in later years the placing of a figurehead at the bow close under the bowsprit made a perfect finish to a wooden merchant ship, particularly the clipper with her beautiful lines culminating at that point.

In Australia the story of figureheads centres around merchantmen, and the Port of Adelaide Museum has the finest collection in Australia. Several of these have been recovered from ships wrecked in South Australian waters and restored. The museum has more than a dozen figureheads in its collection.

General Blanco.

A figure in Scottish costume with an outstretched arm. It was recovered from the ship after she was dismasted off Troubridge Shoal in 1856 and sold to pay the wages of the crew and other expenses.

Sultana.

A Turkish lady dressed in pantaloons, jacket and slippers. Taken from the ship after she was lost at Guichen Bay in 1857.

Star Of Greece.

A lady of dark complexion gazing forward. Was in the possession of W.J. Kimber for many years. After his death his widow presented it to the Nautical Museum. The ship was wrecked at Port Willunga in 1888.

Wave Queen.

A lady holding out a bunch of flowers. This ship was lost at Rivoli Bay in 1874.

Margit

A woman with her left hand at her breast. Taken from the barque wrecked on The Coorong in 1911.

156

This magnificently restored figurehead of the *Star of Greece* is on display at the Maritime Museum in Port Adelaide.
(Author's Collection).

APPENDIX B

SUMMARY OF MAJOR INCIDENTS ALONG THE SOUTH AUSTRALIAN SECTION OF THE MURRAY RIVER.

1842 The cutter *Water Witch* was used to help survey Encounter Bay, then she sailed up the river to the Government Station near Blanchetown. Here she sank on a blustery day in December after leaking badly, and was never refloated. Built at Hobart in 1834, she was a wooden vessel of 25 tons.

P.S.Bunyip was almost totally destroyed by fire on the Murray River near Chowilla Station in 1866.

1866 The *Bunyip* and two barges were completely destroyed by fire about eleven kilometres above Chowilla Station on 8 December. Two members of the crew and a child passenger lost their lives and most others on board suffered burns. The *Bunyip*, 277 tons, was built in 1858 as a double hulled vessel and when rebuilt in 1862 was converted to a single hulled stern-wheeler.

1874 A boiler explosion on the *Moolgewanke* at Swan Reach claimed three lives. The hull was not badly damaged and was converted into a barge which was also destroyed by fire many years later. Built in 1866 she was a vessel of 271 tons.

1880 The steamer *Clara* was burnt to the water's edge at Morgan on 11 June after attempts to scuttle her had failed. She was a vessel of 79 tons, built in 1816.

1882   The *Vesta* struck a sandbar near Overland Corner on 8 July and may have been abandoned, although her register was not closed until 1909. Built in 1867, she was a vessel of 29 tons.

1886   The steamer *Roma,* bound to Goolwa with wool was destroyed by fire near Tailem Bend on 26 December. Apparently the extremely hot weather and heat from the funnel were responsible. She was a vessel of 67 tons, built in 1884.

1888   Fire destroyed the *Britannia* at Cragie Creek on 23 July while she was on her way to Wentworth. Several of the passengers and crew were badly burnt. She was a vessel of 186 tons, built in 1876.

1903   One of the hulls of the *Bunyip* which was destroyed by fire in 1866 was converted into a schooner named *Waterlily* which traded on Lake Alexandrina before sinking off point Malcolm.

1909   The *Hartley* sank opposite the Murray Bridge wharf.

1915   The *Sapphire* was burnt at Renmark.

1928   The *Struggler* was destroyed by fire in March when moored near Mannum. She was used originally to transport livestock and was later fitted out to accommodate fishing parties.

After an eventful life on the river the *Queen* was destroyed by fire at Mypolonga on 13 September. Built in 1865 she was a vessel of 165 tons.

1929   The steamer *Waikerie* was burnt at Morgan on the night of 12 September. Built in 1911 she was a vessel of 82 tons.

1930   The steamer *Coorawa* sank in deep water near Morgan in January,

1951   *P.S.Renmark* was burnt to the water's edge at Goolwa on 2 February shortly after she had been refitted for the tourist trade. Built in 1912 she was a vessel of 152 tons.

1958   The eighteen passenger *Merle,* well known on the Murray for more than 50 years, burned and sank at Murray Bridge on 1 March. She was built in 1904 and measured 87 tons.

1985   The 40 ton houseboat **Proud Mary** was gutted by fire at Murray Bridge.

APPENDIX C

HULKS IN THE NORTH ARM GRAVEYARD, PORT ADELAIDE

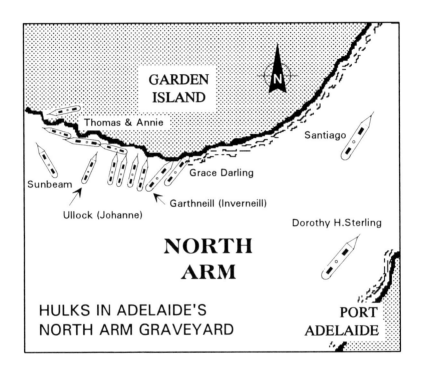

Santiago

The hulk of the iron barque *Santiago* dominates Adelaide's graveyard where the decaying remains of many proud ships have lain for decades.

Built in 1856 by Balfour, Methill, Scotland for E.E.C.Tobias, the *Santiago* was a vessel of 460 tons. She was sailing under the Norwegian flag when bought at Newcastle in 1900 by the Adelaide Steam Tug Company and used as a coal hulk. The Adelaide Steamship Company purchased her in 1918 and she was in service until 1945 when she was partly dismantled and abandoned in the North Arm.

Present day visitors are still able to admire her fine lines and examine the stumps of her three masts and miscellaneous fittings.

There are at least thirteen other derelicts lying nearby; some identified, some not. Among the vessels unidentified are several iron steamers and barges.

The remains of the iron barque *Santiago* is the best known hulk in the North Arm Ship's Graveyard at Port Adelaide.
(Graeme Andrews).

Dorothy H.Sterling

When the Peninsula Ship Building Company of Portland, Oregon commenced her in 1920 she was planned to be a steamer, however, she was completed as a six masted schooner. After arriving in Adelaide in 1927 her owners were declared bankrupt and so she was sold and partly broken up. The lower masts were apparently used as fenders over the wharf at Outer Harbour and three of her topmasts were used as masts on the fore-and-aft schooner *Moorara*. Today, mangroves and other prolific growths have almost completely hidden her.

Flinders

This is probably the 948 ton steamer built in 1878 for the Tasmanian Steam Navigation Company, then later owned by the Union Steam Ship Company of New Zealand. She caught fire at Port Adelaide in 1911 and was converted to a hulk before being dismantled in 1927.

Garthneill (Inverneill)

She arrived in Melbourne in 1925 after a 122 day voyage from Grangemouth, and after being laid up for a short period was sold to the Yorke Peninsula Company who used her to store gypsum, lime and salt at Adelaide. She was finally dismantled in 1935.

Glaucus

An iron steamer of 1363 tons built at Sunderland in 1878, she operated in Australian waters until hulked in the twenties, then was finally broken up about 1934.

Grace Darling

A steel steamer of 622 tons, built in 1907 for J.Darling & Company. Her register was closed in 1931.

Juno

A steel steamer of 241 tons built in 1903 for Coast Steamships Limited. Later she was owned by the Coast Steam Ship Company before her register closed in 1931.

Mangana

An iron vessel of 772 tons, built at Glasgow in 1876 for the Tasmanian Steam Navigation Company. After passing to several owners she was purchased by Huddart Parker Limited at Sydney in 1900. In 1901 she was towed to Adelaide and finally abandoned in the North Arm in March 1931.

Sunbeam

An iron barque of 442 tons, built in 1857. After being hulked in Melbourne in 1886 she was broken up in 1909.

Ullock (Johanne)

An iron barque of 815 tons built at Aberdeen in 1875. Purchased by Huddart Parker for use as a hulk in 1911 and finally broken up in 1937.

Thomas & Annie

A wooden ketch of 15 tons built in Tasmania in 1874. Her register was closed in 1945.

APPENDIX D

HISTORIC SHIPWRECK LEGISLATION

Historic Shipwrecks legislation exists to protect and preserve for the future Australia's most significant shipwrecks. This protection benefits the community by ensuring that wreck sites are not destroyed or damaged by divers. In the long term everyone benefits through displays of relics in museums where the public can learn about their historical or technological significance.

The State Heritage Branch of the Department of Environment and Planning has records for many shipwrecks lying within South Australian waters. The majority have not been accurately positioned and identified. Some have been declared historic under the historic shipwrecks legislation of the State and the Commonwealth.

The shipwrecks located in South Australia represent the range of vessels and industries involved in the discovery, settlement and development of South Australia from 1836 onwards. They include vessels used in the whaling industry, colonial emigration, overseas and coastal transportation, and transportation on the River Murray.

Many of the early international vessels were of the British wooden type replaced by large iron, then steel, sailing vessels and then steamers. The majority of the smaller vessels were built in various parts of Australia and in particular, in Tasmania and South Australia. There are also the remains of associated port facilities and lighthouses scattered around the coast and in the River Murray.

The management of shipwrecks needs the involvement of the community in several aspects such as, discovering sites, research, excavation and conservation. It is also important in this management if artefacts already recovered from shipwrecks are documented so that their identity, significance and display potential is known. Shipwrecks and their associated artefacts require specialised conservation treatments to assist in their preservation for future generations to appreciate.

For further information contact: State Heritage Branch, Department of Environment and Planning, G.P.O.Box 667, Adelaide SA 5001.

APPENDIX E

GLOSSARY

Aft	Towards the stern.
Barge	Name often given to a small flat bottomed sailing craft.
Barque	Three or four-masted ship with fore and aft sails on the mizzen mast.
Barquentine	Three-masted ship carrying square rigging on the fore-mast only, and staysails between the fore and main masts.
Beam	Width of a ship.
Bilge	Section along the ship's bottom where it curves into the sides. Drainage well alongside the holds and the water it collects.
Binnacle	Cover over the ship's compass.
Bollards	Metal or wooden posts for the securing of ropes.
Boom	Used to extend or support a sail.
Bower anchor	Heavy anchor used to anchor the ship.
Brig	Two-masted vessel with square sails on each mast, also fore and aft staysails and jibs.
Brigantine	Two-masted vessel with the foremast square rigged and the mainmast fore and aft rigged.
Bulwarks	Solid, planked rail, about a metre above the weather deck for the crew's safety. Also helps secure deck cargo and keeps out some of the sea in rough weather.
Clipper	A sailing vessel width raking bow and sloping masts.
Companion	A skylight or window to admit light into a cabin.
Falls	Tackle used to lower lifeboat.
Fenders	Pieces fixed to the side of the ship to prevent damage.
Fore	Near the bow.
Foremast	Mast closest to the bow.
Founder	To sink.
Halyards	Ropes and tackles for hoisting sails and yards.
Head Sheets	Sails forewarn of the foremast; usually fore and aft type, often called jibs.
Head Stays	Supporting ropes and wires near the bow.
Helm	Ship's steering gear.

Jibboom	A spar run out from the bowsprit.
Jolly Boat	Used for minor tasks.
Jury Sail	A makeshift sail usually used in an emergency.
Kedge	A small anchor used during mooring or moving of the ship.
Knot	A unit of speed equal to one nautical mile.
Lee Side	Away from the wind.
Luff	Allowing the vessel to come up into the wind, thus relieving pressure on the sails.
Mainmast	Tallest or principal mast.
Missed Stays	Failure of the attempt to make the ship go about.
Mizzen Mast	Third mast aft where there are more than two masts.
Port	Left side, looking towards the bow.
Rapier	A slender sword.
Register and Articles	
	Documents containing details of the ship.
Roaring Forties	Latitude 40' to 50' South, the area of strong westerlies.
Royals	Square sails immediately above the top gallant sails.
Sails Aback	When yards are trimmed so wind is on their forward side tending to drive the vessel astern.
Sails Clewed	Bringing the yard down when the sail is filled; letting go the halyards.
Sails Furled	Securing sails on the yard or boom by rolling up.
Saloon	Dining and recreation room.
Schooner	A vessel with fore and aft sails.
Sheets	Ropes attached to the lower corners of a sail.
Sheet Anchor	Large anchor kept for emergencies.
Starboard	Right side looking towards the bow.
Staysails	Triangular sails hoisted upon a stay.
Stern Sheets	Boards or rear space in a rowing boat.
Stream Anchor	A working anchor, weighing between a kedge and a bower.
Tonnage Gross	Cubic capacity including wheelhouse, galley, stairways.
Tonnage Net Register	
	Measure of space available for passengers and cargo.
Tonnage Displacement	
	Weight of water the ship displaces.
Topgallants	Square sails above the topsails on a square rigged ship.

Topsail	Second lowermost square sail carried by some ships; usually combined with a topgallant sail on a foremast.
Unbend	To loosen.
Wear Ship	To change the tack by turning the head away from the wind.
Weather Deck	The uppermost deck on a ship.
Yards	Spars slung at their centres from the mast supporting and extending a square sail.

Anchor from the *Ethel* displayed on the site of the wreck.
(Author's Collection).

INDEX - SHIPS

INDEX - SHIPS

INDEX - SHIPS

INDEX - PLACES

INDEX - PLACES

INDEX - PLACES

INDEX - PLACES

INDEX - PLACES

INDEX- GENERAL

INDEX - GENERAL

INDEX - PEOPLE

INDEX - PEOPLE

INDEX - PEOPLE